SACRED WISDOM

TALES FROM
RUMI

Essential Selections from
The Mathnawi

Translated by
E.H. Whinfield

Introduction to this edition
by Alan Jacobs

WATKINS PUBLISHING

LONDON

This selection is taken from
*The Mathnawi, The Spiritual Couplets of
Maulána Jalálu-'D-Dín Muhammad I Rúmí*
translated and abridged by E.H. Whinfield MA
first published *c* 1900

This edition produced in 2006 for Sacred Wisdom,
an imprint of Watkins Publishing
Sixth Floor, Castle House, 75–76 Wells Street,
London W1T 3QH

Distributed in the United States and Canada by
Sterling Publishing Co., Inc.
387 Park Avenue South, New York, NY 10016-8810

1 3 5 7 9 10 8 6 4 2

Designed in Great Britain by Jerry Goldie
Typeset in Great Britain by Dorchester Typesetting Group
Printed and bound in Thailand by Imago

Library of Congress Cataloging-in-Publication data available

ISBN-10: 1-84293-122-9
ISBN-13: 9-781842-931226

www.watkinspublishing.com

CONTENTS

PUBLISHER'S NOTE

The translation of *The Mathnawi* by E.H. Whinfield is presented with a short prose summary of each story followed by two or three samples of Rumi's original verse, with subheadings to explain which part of the story is being described. The page numbers after the story titles and subheadings refer to the original Lucknow edition of *The Mathnawi*.

INTRODUCTION

*The rose of Gnosis fostered by the sun of rapture
and the moon of overflowing Grace in the Garden
of the Mathnawi.*

Sari al-Saqati

*Let us salute the great glories of the Mathnawi[1]
by the celebrated Jalalu'-ddin Rumi.*

R.A. Nicholson

The *Mathnawi* is universally revered as one of the most important and longest mystical poems ever written, containing 24,000 verses in rhyming couplets. In the words of the esteemed Persian scholar Reynold Nicholson, "It is a mystic river, calm and deep, meandering through many a rich and varied landscape to the immeasurable ocean."

Jalalu'ddin Rumi was born at Balkh in Afghanistan in 1207. His father, after a dispute with the local monarch, moved to Nishapur. It was here that the celebrated Sufi poet Faridu'd-Din Attar presented the young Rumi with his famed *Book of Mysteries* and informed his father that one day his son would be renowned throughout the world. His prophetic words have come true, for today the poems of Rumi are some of the most popular, most translated and most widely read poems in the English-speaking world, particularly in America.

Eventually the family moved to Konya in Turkey, an old Roman province, and so Jalalu'ddin was nicknamed Rumi or "the Roman". Rumi was a child prodigy. At the age of six he had visions of the celestial regions and taught his playmates philosophy as a game. On the death of his father he took a professorial chair and soon founded the famed order of Dervishes, the Mevlevi. He authorised music and dancing in their ceremonies, and because of their ecstatic turning they became known as the Whirling Dervishes. Rumi believed that through this dance the soul could be released from the prison of the body and wing its way back to its source. He believed that we should drown in the Ocean of Divine Love.

As Arthur Symons, the Victorian poet, wrote in praise of the Dervishes:

I turn until my senses
Dazzled with waves of air
Spin to a point intense
And spiral and centre there.

In 1226 Jalalu'ddin married his precious sweetheart, Pearl. They had two sons. Tragically Pearl died early in her life. Rumi remarried, and his second wife fortunately survived him.

A mysterious Being, "un homme inconnu" called Shams Tabriz, met Rumi in unknown circumstances. The poet instantly recognised Shams as a God-Realised Soul and became his pupil. It was Shams who brought Rumi to God-Realisation.

Rumi wrote a set of ecstatic love poems, The Divani, for Shams, whom he equated with the Self or the Divine Beloved, "a foaming torrent that leaps and plunges in the solitude of the mountains."[2] Rumi's disciples became jealous of Shams because of their Master's adoration, and he met a violent death from an unknown hand. An envious pupil was suspected. Rumi and Shams had both surrendered to the Divine and accepted God's will in whatever happened.

The Arabic historian Al-Aflaki relates numerous stories recounting the miracles of Rumi and his wise aphorisms. Rumi loved all children, whom he saw as potential citizens of God on our planet. He died in Konya in 1223. To this day pilgrims visit his shrine, and his order of Dervishes continues his teaching and turning practice, touring worldwide.

Rumi's major work, this *Mathnawi*, was written over three years. Whole nights were spent in inspired dictation to his scribe, Hasan. It is written in rhyming couplets and this edition, translated in 1887 by the renowned Persian scholar E.H. Whinfield, has been further abridged and fully captures the spirit of the original. The poetry was included by Rumi within each narrative. *The Mathnawi* is a cornucopia of profound mysteries; it acts as a bible for the Sufis and is a source of inspiration for many in all the major religions who tread the mystical path.

The essence of this book filled with ecstatic poetry and wise stories is the singing of the soul's longing to be united with the Beloved. It often makes full use of bacchanalian and erotic symbolism. It conveys the music of the mountains, the calm of the valleys, the fragrances of the rose garden, the flow of the rivers, the flight of the birds and the swaying of the trees in prayer.

In Rumi's own words, "This book contains the roots of the Faith and treats of the mysteries of Union and Certitude."

Many who have found themselves in the darkest depths of depression have been brought back into joyous appreciation of life and its purpose through this monumental work of sublime narrative and exquisite poetry.

Alan Jacobs

Notes

1. Mathnawi means "poems in rhymed couplets". The Persian language abounds in "a" endings so the task of creating these is relatively easier than in other tongues.
2. R.A. Nicholson.

BOOK I

THE PRINCE AND
THE HANDMAID (P. 5)

A prince, while engaged on a hunting excursion, espied a fair maiden, and by promises of gold induced her to accompany him. After a time she fell sick, and the prince had her tended by divers physicians. As, however, they all omitted to say, "*God willing*,[1] we will cure her," their treatment was of no avail. So the prince offered prayer, and in answer thereto a physician was sent from heaven. He at once condemned his predecessors' view of the case, and by a very skilful diagnosis, discovered that the real cause of the maiden's illness was her love for a certain goldsmith of Samarcand. In accordance with the physician's advice, the prince sent to Samarcand and fetched the goldsmith, and married him to the lovesick maiden, and for six months the pair lived together in

the utmost harmony and happiness. At the end of that
period the physician, by divine command, gave the
goldsmith a poisonous draught, which caused his
strength and beauty to decay, and he then lost favour
with the maiden, and she was reunited to the king. This
Divine command was precisely similar to God's
command to Abraham to slay his son Ishmael, and to the
act of the angel in slaying the servant of Moses,[2] and is
therefore beyond human criticism.

Description of love (P. 7)

A true lover is proved such by his pain of heart;
No sickness is there like sickness of heart.
The lover's ailment is different from all ailments;
Love is the astrolabe of God's mysteries.
A lover may hanker after this love or that love,
But at the last he is drawn to the KING of love.
However much we describe and explain love,
When we fall in love we are ashamed of our words.
Explanation by the tongue makes most things clear,
But love unexplained is clearer.

When pen hasted to write,

On reaching the subject of love it split in twain.

When the discourse touched on the matter of love,

Pen was broken and paper torn.

In explaining it Reason sticks fast, as an ass in mire;

Naught but Love itself can explain love and lovers!

None but the sun can display the sun,

If you would see it displayed, turn not away from it.

Shadows, indeed, may indicate the sun's presence,

But only the sun displays the light of life.

Shadows induce slumber, like evening talks,

But when the sun arises the "moon is split
    asunder."[3]

In the world there is naught so wondrous as the sun,

But the Sun of the soul sets not and has no
    yesterday.

Though the material sun is unique and single,

We can conceive similar suns like to it.

But the Sun of the soul, beyond this firmament,—

No like thereof is seen in concrete or abstract.[4]

Where is there room in conception for HIS essence,

So that similitudes of HIM should be conceivable?

Shamsu-'d-Din of Tabriz importunes
Jalalu-'d-Din to compose the Mathnawi (P. 7)

The sun (*Shams*) of Tabriz is a perfect light,
A sun, yea, one of the beams of God!
When the praise was heard of the "Sun of Tabriz,"
The sun of the fourth heaven bowed its head.
Now that I have mentioned his name, it is but right
To set forth some indications of his beneficence.
That precious Soul caught my skirt,
Smelling the perfume of the garment of Yusuf;
And said, "For the sake of our ancient friendship,
Tell forth a hint of those sweet states of ecstasy,
That earth and heaven may be rejoiced,
And also Reason and Spirit, a hundredfold."
I said, "O thou who art far from 'The Friend,'
Like a sick man who has strayed from his physician,
Importune me not, for I am beside myself;
My understanding is gone, I cannot sing praises.
Whatsoever one says, whose reason is thus astray,
Let him not boast; his efforts are useless.
Whatever he says is not to the point,

And is clearly inapt and wide of the mark.

What can I say when not a nerve of mine is
    sensible?

Can I explain 'The Friend' to one to whom He is
    no Friend?

Verily my singing His praise were dispraise,

For 'twould prove me existent, and existence is
    error.[5]

Can I describe my separation and my bleeding heart?

Nay, put off this matter till another season."

He said, "Feed me, for I am an hungred,

And at once, for 'the time is a sharp sword.'

O comrade, the Sufi is 'the son of time present.'[6]

It is not the rule of his canon to say, 'To-morrow.'

Can it be that thou art not a true Sufi?

Ready money is lost by giving credit."

I said, "'Tis best to veil the secrets of 'The Friend.'

So give good heed to the morals of these stories.

That is better than that the secrets of 'The Friend'

Should be noised abroad in the talk of strangers."

He said, "Without veil or covering or deception,

Speak out, and vex me not, O man of many words!

Strip off the veil and speak out, for do not I

Enter under the same coverlet as the Beloved?"

I said, "If the Beloved were exposed to outward
    view,

Neither wouldst thou endure, nor embrace, nor
    form.

Press thy suit, yet with moderation;

A blade of grass cannot pierce a mountain.

If the sum that illumines the world

Were to draw nigher, the world would be
    consumed.[7]

Close thy mouth and shut the eyes of this matter,

That the world's life be not made a bleeding heart.

No longer seek this peril, this bloodshed;

Hereafter impose silence on the 'Sun of Tabriz.'"

He said, "Thy words are endless. Now tell forth

All thy story from its beginning."

Notes

1. As enjoined in Koran xviii. 23. One cannot converse with a
   strict Musulman for five minutes without hearing the
   formula, "*In sha Allah Ta'alla*," or *D.V.*

2. Koran xviii. 73.

3. Koran liv. 1.

4. There is a tradition, "I know my Lord by my Lord."
5. See Gulshan i Ras, l. 400. In the state of union self remains not.
6. The Sufi is the "son of the time present," because he is an Energumen, or passive instrument moved by the divine impulse of the moment. "The time present is a sharp sword," because the divine impulse of the moment dominates the Energumen, and executes its decrees sharply. See Sohravardi quoted in *Notices et Extraits des MSS.*, xii. 371 note.
7. "When its Lord appears in glory to the Mount of existence, Existence is laid low, like the dust of the road." – Gulshan i Raz, l. 195.

THE LION AND
THE BEASTS (P. 26)

In the book of Kalila and Damna a story is told of a lion who held all the beasts of the neighbourhood in subjection, and was in the habit of making constant raids upon them, to take and kill such of them as he required for his daily food. At last the beasts took counsel together, and agreed to deliver up one of their company every day, to satisfy the lion's hunger, if he, on his part, would cease to annoy them by his continual forays. The lion was at first unwilling to trust to their promise, remarking that he always preferred to rely on his own exertions; but the beasts succeeded in persuading him that he would do well to trust Providence and their word. To illustrate the thesis that human exertions are vain, they related a story of a man who got Solomon to transport him to Hindustan to escape the angel of death, but was smitten by the angel the moment he got there. Having carried their point, the beasts continued for some time to perform their engagement. One day it came to the turn of the hare to be delivered up as a victim to the lion; but he requested the others to let him practise a stratagem. They scoffed at him, asking how such a silly beast as he could pretend to outwit the lion. The hare assured them that wisdom was of God, and God might choose weak things to confound the strong. At last they consented to let him try his luck. He took his way slowly to the lion, and found him sorely enraged. In excuse for his tardy arrival he represented that he and another hare had set out together to appear before the lion, but a strange lion had seized the second hare, and carried it off in spite of his remonstrances. On hearing this the lion was exceeding wroth, and commanded the hare to show him the foe who had trespassed on his preserves. Pretending to be afraid, the hare got the lion to take him upon his back, and directed him to a well. On looking down the well, the lion saw in the water the reflection of himself and of the hare on his back; and thinking that he saw his foe with the stolen hare, he plunged in to attack him, and was drowned, while the hare sprang off his back

and escaped. This folly on the part of the lion was predestined to punish him for denying God's ruling
providence. So Adam, though he knew the name of all
things, in accordance with God's predestination,
neglected to obey a single prohibition, and his dis-
obedience cost him dearly.

*Trust in God, as opposed to
human exertions* (P. 26)

The beasts said, "O enlightened sage,

Lay aside caution; it cannot help thee against
destiny;

To worry with precaution is toil and moil;

Go, trust in Providence, trust is the better part.

War not with the divine decree, O hot-headed one,

Lest that decree enter into conflict with thee.

Man should be as dead before the commands of God,

Lest a blow befall him from the Lord of all
creatures."

He said, "True; but though trust be our mainstay,

Yet the Prophet teaches us to have regard to means.

The Prophet cried with a loud voice,

'Trust in God, yet tie the camel's leg.'[1]

Hear the adage, 'The worker is the friend of God;'[2]

Through trust in Providence neglect not to use
   means.

Go, O Quietists, practise trust with self-exertion,

Exert yourself to attain your objects, bit by bit.

In order to succeed, strive and exert yourselves;

If ye strive not for your objects, ye are fools."

They said, "What is gained from the poor by
   exertions

Is a fraudulent morsel that will bring ill luck.

Again, know that self-exertion springs from
   weakness;

Relying on other means is a blot upon perfect trust.

Self-exertion is not more noble than trust in God.

What is more lovely than committing oneself to
   God?

Many there are who flee from one danger to a worse;

Many flee from a snake and meet a dragon.

Man plans a stratagem, and thereby snares himself;

What he takes for life turns out to be destruction.

He shuts the door after his foe is in the house.

After this sort were the schemes of Pharaoh.

That jealous king slew a myriad babes,

While Moses, whom he sought, was in his house.

Our eyes are subject to many infirmities;

Go! annihilate your sight in God's sight.

For our foresight His foresight is a fair exchange;

In His sight is all that ye can desire.

So long as a babe cannot grasp or run,

It takes its father's back for its carriage.

But when it becomes independent and uses its hands,

It falls into grievous troubles and disgrace.

The souls of our first parents, even before their hands,

Flew away from fidelity after vain pleasure.

Being made captives by the command, 'Get down hence,'[3]

They become bond-slaves of enmity, lust, and vanity.

We are the family of the Lord and His sucking babes.

The Prophet said, 'The people are God's family;'

He who sends forth the rain from heaven,

Can He not also provide us our daily bread?"
The lion said, "True; yet the Lord of creatures
Sets a ladder before our feet.
Step by step must we mount up to the roof!
The notion of fatalism is groundless in this place.
Ye have feet – why then pretend ye are lame?
Ye have hands – why then conceal your claws?
When a master places a spade in the hand of a slave,
The slave knows his meaning without being told.
Like this spade, our hands are our Master's hints
    to us;
Yea, if ye consider, they are His directions to us.
When ye have taken to heart His hints,
Ye will shape your life in reliance on their direction;
Wherefore these hints disclose His intent,
Take the burden from you, and appoint your work.
He that bears it makes it bearable by you,
He that is able makes it within your ability.
Accept His command, and you will be able to
    execute it;
Seek union with Him, and you will find yourselves
    united.

Exertion is giving thanks for God's blessings;
Think ye that your fatalism gives such thanks?
Giving thanks for blessings increases blessings,
But fatalism snatches those blessings from your
    hands.
Your fatalism is to sleep on the road; sleep not
Till ye behold the gates of the King's palace.
Ah! sleep not, O unreflecting fatalists,
Till ye have reached that fruit-laden Tree of Life
Whose branches are ever shaken by the wind,
And whose fruit is showered on the sleepers' heads.
Fatalism means sleeping amidst highwaymen.
Can a cock who crows too soon expect peace?
If ye cavil at and accept not God's hints,
Though ye count yourselves men, see, ye are
    women.
The quantum of reason ye possessed is lost,
And the head whose reason has fled is a tail.
Inasmuch as the unthankful are despicable,
They are at last cast into the fiery pit.
If ye really have trust in God, exert yourselves,
And strive, in constant reliance on the Almighty."

*Wisdom is granted oftentimes to
the weak* (P. 29)

He said, "O friends, God has given me inspiration.

Oftentimes strong counsel is suggested to the weak.

The wit taught by God to the bee

Is withheld from the lion and the wild ass.

It fills its cells with liquid sweets,

For God opens the door of this knowledge to it.

The skill taught by God to the silkworm

Is a learning beyond the reach of the elephant.

The earthly Adam was taught of God names,[4]

So that his glory reached the seventh heaven.

He laid low the name and fame of the angels,[5]

Yet blind indeed are they whom God dooms to
doubt!

The devotee of seven hundred thousand years
(Satan)

Was made a muzzle for that yearling calf (Adam),[6]

Lest he should suck milk of the knowledge of faith,

And soar on high even to the towers of heaven.

The knowledge of men of external sense is a muzzle

To stop them sucking milk of that sublime
    knowledge.

But God drops into the heart a single pearl-drop

Which is not bestowed on oceans or skies!"

"How long regard ye mere form, O form-
    worshippers?

Your souls, void of substance, rest still in forms.

If the form of man were all that made man,

Ahmad and Abu Jahl would be upon a par.

A painting on a wall resembles a man,

But see what it is lacking in that empty form.

'Tis life that is lacking to that mere semblance of
    man.

Go! seek for that pearl it never will find.

The heads of earth's lions were bowed down

When God gave might to the Seven Sleepers' dogs.[7]

What mattered its despised form

When its soul was drowned in the sea of light?"

*Human wisdom the manifestation of
divine* (P. 31)

On his way to the lion the hare lingered,
Devising a stratagem with himself.
He proceeded on his way after delaying long,
In order to have a secret or two for the lion.
What worlds the principle of Reason embraces!
How broad is this ocean of Reason!
Yea, the Reason of man is a boundless ocean.
O son, that ocean requires, as it were, a diver.[8]
On this fair ocean our human forms
Float about, like bowls on the surface of water;
Yea, like cups on the surface, till they are filled;
And when filled, these cups sink into the water.
The ocean of Reason is not seen; reasoning men are
     seen;
But our forms (minds) are only as waves or spray
     thereof.
Whatever form that ocean uses as its instrument,
Therewith it casts its spray far and wide.[9]
Till the heart sees the Giver of the secret,

Till it espies that Bowman shooting from afar,

It fancies its own steed lost, while in bewilderment

It is urging that steed hither and thither;[10]

It fancies its own steed lost, when all the while

That swift steed is bearing it on like the wind.

In deep distress that blunderhead

Runs from door to door, searching and inquiring,

"Who and where is he that hath stolen my steed?"

They say, "What is this thou ridest on, O master?"

He says, "True, 'tis a steed; but where is mine?"

They say, "Look to thyself, O rider; thy steed is
    there."

The real Soul is lost to view, and seems far off;[11]

Thou art like a pitcher with full belly but dry lip;

How canst thou ever see red, green, and scarlet

Unless thou see'st the light first of all?

When thy sight is dazzled by colours,

These colours veil the light from thee.

But when night veils those colours from thee,

Thou seest that colours are seen only through light.

As there is no seeing outward colours without light,

So it is with the mental colours within.

Outward colours arise from the light of sun and
    stars,

And inward colours from the Light on high.

The light that lights the eye is also the heart's Light;

The eye's light proceeds from the Light of the heart,

But the light that lights the heart is the Light of
    God,

Which is distinct from the light of reason and sense.

At night there is no light, and colours are not seen;

Hence we know what light is by its opposite,
    darkness.

At night no colours are visible, for light is lacking.

How can colour be the attribute of dark blackness?

Looking on light is the same as looking on colours;

Opposite shows up opposite, as a Frank a Negro.

The opposite of light shows what is light,

Hence colours too are known by their opposite.

God created pain and grief for this purpose,

To wit, to manifest happiness by its opposites.[12]

Hidden things are manifested by their opposites;

But, as God has no opposite, He remains hidden.

God's light has no opposite in the range of creation

Whereby it may be manifested to view.

Perforce "Our eyes see not Him, though He sees us."[13]

Behold this in the case of Moses and Mount Sinai.[14]

Discern form from substance, as lion from desert,

Or as sound and speech from the thought they convey.

The sound and speech arise from the thought;

Thou knowest not where is the Ocean of thought;

Yet when thou seest fair waves of speech,

Thou knowest there is a glorious Ocean beneath them.

When waves of thought arise from the Ocean of Wisdom,

They assume the forms of sound and speech.

These forms of speech are born and die again,

These waves cast themselves back into the Ocean.

Form is born of That which is without form,

And goes again, for, "Verily to Him do we return."[15]

Wherefore to thee every moment come death and "return."

Mustafa saith, "The world endureth only a moment."

So, thought is an arrow shot by God into the air.

How can it stay in the air? It returns to God.

Every moment the world and we are renewed,[16]

Yet we are ignorant of this renewing for ever and
 aye.

Life, like a stream of water, is renewed and renewed,

Though it wears the appearance of continuity in
 form.

That seeming continuity arises from its swift
 renewal,

As when a single spark of fire is whirled round
 swiftly.[17]

If a single spark be whirled round swiftly,

It seems to the eye a continuous line of fire.

This apparent extension, owing to the quick motion,

Demonstrates the rapidity with which it is moved.

If ye seek the deepest student of this mystery,

Lo! 'tis Husamu-'d-Din, the most exalted of
 creatures!

Notes

1. "Trust in God and keep your powder dry."
2. "Laborare est orare."
3. Koran ii. 341.

4. "And He taught Adam the names of all things"
   (Koran ii. 29).

5. The angels said, "We have no knowledge but what thou
   hast given us to know" (Koran ii. 30).

6. See Gulshan i Raz, 1. 543.

7. Koran xviii, 17.

8. See Gulshan i Raz, 1. 575: The ocean of Reason is the same
   as what is elsewhere called the ocean of Being, viz., the
   Noumenon, or Divine substratum of all phenomenal being
   and thought.

9. "Those arrows were God's, not yours" (Koran viii. 17); *i.e.*,
   Man's reason proceeds from God, the "Only Real Agent."

10. Alluding to the "Believer's lost camel" (Book Two, Story
    Twelve, *infra*). Men seek wisdom, and do not know that in
    themselves is the reflected wisdom of God (Gulshan
    i Raz, 1. 435).

11. The real Soul, *i.e.*, the spirit which God "breathed into
    man" (Koran xv. 29). "In yourselves are signs; will ye not
    behold them?" (Koran li. 21).

12. See Gulshan i Raz, l. 92. Mr Mansel (Bampton Lectures,
    p. 49) says: "A thing can be known as that which it is only
    by being distinguished from that which it is not." But the
    Infinite Deity *ex hypothesi* includes all things; so there is
    nothing to contrast Him with.

13. Koran vi. 103.

14. Koran vii. 139: "He said, 'Thou shalt not see me.'"

15. Koran ii, 151.

16. See Gulshan i Raz, 1. 645: All phenomena are every
    moment renewed by fresh effluxes of being from the
    Divine Noumenon.

17. See Gulshan i Raz, 1. 710.

STORY SIX

'OMAR AND THE
AMBASSADOR (P. 38)

The hare, having delivered his companions from the tyranny of the lion, in the manner just described, proceeds to improve the occasion by exhorting them to engage in a greater and more arduous warfare, viz., the struggle against their inward enemy, the lusts of the flesh. He illustrates his meaning by the story of an ambassador who was sent by the Emperor of Rum to the Khalifa 'Omar. On approaching Medina this ambassador inquired for 'Omar's palace, and learned that 'Omar dwelt in no material palace, but in a spiritual tabernacle, only visible to purified hearts. At last he discerned 'Omar lying under a palm-tree, and drew near to him in fear and awe. 'Omar received him kindly, and instructed him in the doctrine of the mystical union with God. The ambassador heard him gladly, and asked him two questions, first, How can

souls descend from heaven to earth? and secondly, With
what object are souls imprisoned in the bonds of flesh
and blood? 'Omar responded, and the ambassador
accepted his teaching, and became a pure-hearted Sufi.
The hare urged his companions to abjure lust and pride,
and to go and do likewise.

God's agency reconciled with man's free will (P. 39)

The ambassador said, "O Commander of the faithful,
How comes the soul down from above to earth?
How can so noble a bird be confined in a cage?"
He said, "God speaks words of power to souls,—
To things of naught, without eyes or ears,
And at these words they all spring into motion;
At His words of power these nothings arise quickly,
And strong impulse urges them into existence.
Again, He speaks other spells to these creatures,
And swiftly drives them back again into Not-being.
He speaks to the rose's ear, and causes it to bloom;
He speaks to the tulip, and makes it blossom.

He speaks a spell to body, and it becomes soul;

He speaks to the sun, and it becomes a fount of
light.

Again, in its ear He whispers a word of power,

And its face is darkened as by a hundred eclipses.

What is it that God says to the ear of earth,

That it attends thereto and rests steadfast?

What is it that Speaker says to the cloud,

That it pours forth rain-water like a water-skin?

Whosoever is bewildered by wavering will,[1]

In his ear hath God whispered His riddle,

That He may bind him on the horns of a dilemma;

For he says, 'Shall I do this or its reverse?'

Also from God comes the preference of one
alternative;

'Tis from God's impulsion that man chooses one of
the two.

If you desire sanity in this embarrassment,

Stuff not the ear of your mind with cotton.

Take the cotton of evil suggestions from the mind's
ear,[2]

That the heavenly voice from above may enter it,

That you may understand that riddle of His,

That you may be cognisant of that open secret.

Then the mind's ear becomes the sensorium of
   inspiration;

For what is this Divine voice but the inward voice?[3]

The spirit's eye and ear possess this sense,

The eye and ear of reason and sense lack it.

The word 'compulsion' makes me impatient for love's
   sake;

'Tis he who loves not who is fettered by compulsion.

This is close communion with God, not compulsion,

The shining of the sun, and not a dark cloud.

Or, if it be compulsion, 'tis not common compulsion,

It is not the domination of wanton wilfulness.

O son, they understand this compulsion

For whom God opens the eyes of the inner man.

Things hidden and things future are plain to them;

To speak of the past seems to them despicable.

They possess freewill and compulsion besides,[4]

As in oyster-shells raindrops are pearls.

Outside the shell they are raindrops, great and small;

Inside they are precious pearls, big and little.

These men also resemble the musk deer's bag;

Outside it is blood, but inside pure musk;
Yet, say not that outside 'twas mere blood,
Which on entering the bag becomes musk.
Nor say that outside the alembic 'twas mere copper,
And becomes gold inside, when mixed with elixir.
In you freewill and compulsion are vain fancies,
But in them they are the light of Almighty power.
On the table bread is a mere lifeless thing,
When taken into the body it is a life-giving spirit.
This transmutation occurs not in the table's heart,
'Tis soul effects this transmutation with water of
   life.
Such is the power of the soul, O man of right views!
Then what is the power of the Soul of souls? (God).
Bread is the food of the body, yet consider,
How can it be the food of the soul, O son?
Flesh-born man by force of soul
Cleaves mountains with tunnels and mines.
The might of Ferhad's soul cleft a hill;
The might of the Soul's soul cleaves the moon.[5]
If the heart opens the mouth of mystery's store,
The soul springs up swiftly to highest heaven.

If tongue discourses of hidden mysteries,

It kindles a fire that consumes the world.

Behold, then, God's action and man's action;

Know, action does belong to us; this is evident.

If no actions proceeded from men,

How could you say, 'Why act ye thus?'

The agency of God is the cause of our action,

Our actions are the signs of God's agency;

Nevertheless our actions are freely willed by us,

Whence our recompense is either hell or 'The
   Friend.'"

Notes

1. The poet's insistence on the doctrine of God being the *Fá'il
   i Hakíki*, or Only Real Agent, without whose word no being
   and no action can be, leads him to the question of free will
   and compulsion of man's will (see Gulshan i Raz, 1. 555).
2. So Gulshan i Raz, 1. 442.
3. The leading principle of all mysticism is that, independently
   of sense and reason, man possesses an inward sense, or
   intuition, which conveys to him a knowledge of God by
   direct apprehension (see Gulshan i Raz, 1. 431).
4. Their wills are identified with God's will, as in the case of
   the saint Daqúqi (*infra*, Book Three, Story Twelve).
5. As a sign of the last day (Koran liv. 1).

STORY EIGHT

THE HARPER (P. 50)

In the time of the Khalifa 'Omar there lived a harper, whose voice was as sweet as that of the angel Isráfil, and who was in great request at all feasts. But he grew old, and his voice broke, and no one would employ him any longer. In despair he went to the burial-ground of Yathrub, and there played his harp to God, looking to Him for recompense. Having finished his melody he fell asleep, and dreamed he was in heaven. The same night a divine voice came to 'Omar, directing him to go to the burial-ground, and relieve an old man whom he should find there. 'Omar proceeded to the place, found the harper, and gave him money, promising him more when he should need it. The harper cast away his harp, saying that it had diverted him from God, and expressed great contrition for his past sins. 'Omar then instructed him that his worldly journey was now over, and that he must not give way to contrition for the past, as he was now entered into the state of ecstasy and intoxication of union with God, and in this exalted state regard to past and future should be swept away. The harper acted on his instructions, and sang no more.

Apology for applying the term "Bride" to God (P. 52)

Mustafa became beside himself at that sweet call,

His prayer failed on "the night of the early morning halt."

He lifted not head from that blissful sleep,"[1]

So that his morning prayer was put off till noon.

On that, his wedding night, in presence of his bride,

His pure soul attained to kiss her hands.

Love and mistress are both veiled and hidden,

Impute it not as a fault if I call Him "Bride."

I would have kept silence from fear of my Beloved,

If He had granted me but a moment's respite.

But He said, "Speak on, 'tis no fault,

'Tis naught but the necessary result of the hidden
    decree,

'Tis a fault only to him who only sees faults.

How can the Pure Hidden Spirit notice faults?"

Faults seem so to ignorant creatures,

Not in the sight of the Lord of Benignity.

Blasphemy even may be wisdom in the Creator's
    sight,

Whereas from our point of view it is grievous sin.

If one fault occur among a hundred beauties,

'Tis as one dry stick in a garden of green herbs.

Both weigh equally in the scales,

For the two resemble body and soul.

Wherefore the sages have said not idly,

"The bodies of the righteous are as pure souls."

Their words, their actions, their praises,

Are all as a pure soul without spot or blemish.

*'Omar rebukes the harper for brooding
over and bewailing the past* (P. 57)

Then 'Omar said to him, "This wailing of thine

Shows thou art still in a state of 'sobriety.'"

Afterwards he thus urged him to quit that state,

And called him out of his beggary to absorption
in God:

"Sobriety savours of memory of the past;

Past and future are what veil God from our sight.

Burn up both of them with fire! How long

Wilt thou be partitioned by these segments as a
reed?

So long as a reed has partitions 'tis not privy to
secrets,

Nor is it vocal in response to lip and breathing.

While circumambulating the house thou art a
stranger;

When thou enterest in thou art at home.

Thou whose knowledge is ignorance of the Giver
of knowledge,

Thy wailing contrition is worse than thy sin.

The road of the 'annihilated' is another road;

Sobriety is wrong, and a straying from that other
    road.

O thou who seekest to be contrite for the past,

How wilt thou be contrite for this contrition?

At one time thou adorest the music of the lute,

At another embracest wailing and weeping."

While the "Discerner" reflected these mysteries,

The heart of the harper was emancipated.

Like a soul he was freed from weeping and rejoicing,

His old life died, and he was regenerated.

Amazement fell upon him at that moment,

For he was exalted above earth and heaven,

An uplifting of the heart surpassing all uplifting;—

I cannot describe it; if you can, say on!

Ecstasy and words beyond all ecstatic words;—

Immersion in the glory of the Lord of glory!

Immersion wherefrom was no extrication,—

As it were identification with the Very Ocean!

Partial Reason is as naught to Universal Reason,

If one impulse dependent on another impulse be
   naught;

But when *that* impulse moves *this* impulse,

The waves of *that* sea rise to *this* point.[2]

Notes

1. The night of his marriage with Safiyya.
2. *I.e.*, he is possessed by the Deity as an "Energumen," and
   the Deity works these ecstatic states in him.

STORY TEN

THE MAN WHO WAS
TATTOOED (P. 74)

It was the custom of the men of Qazwin to have various devices tattooed upon their bodies. A certain coward went to the artist to have such a device tattooed on his back, and desired that it might be the figure of a lion. But when he felt the pricks of the needles he roared with pain, and said to the artist, "What part of the lion are you now painting?" The artist replied, "I am doing the tail." The patient cried, "Never mind the tail; go on with another part." The artist accordingly began in another part, but the patient again cried out and told him to try somewhere else. Wherever the artist applied his needles, the patient raised similar objections, till at last the artist dashed all his needles and pigments on the ground, and refused to proceed any further.

*The Prophet's counsels to 'Ali to follow the
direction of the Pir or Spiritual Guide,
and to endure his chastisements patiently* (P. 75)

The Prophet said to 'Ali, "O 'Ali,

Thou art the Lion of God, a hero most valiant;

Yet confide not in thy lion-like valour,

But seek refuge under the palm-trees of the 'Truth.'

Whoso takes obedience as his exemplar

Shares its proximity to the ineffable Presence.

Do thou seek to draw near to Reason; let not thy
heart

Rely, like others, on thy own virtue and piety.

Come under the shadow of the Man of Reason,[1]

Thou canst not find it in the road of the
traditionists.

That man enjoys close proximity to Allah;

Turn not away from obedience to him in any wise;

For he makes the thorn a bed of roses,

And gives sight to the eyes of the blind.

His shadow on earth is as that of Mount Qáf,

His spirit is as a Simurgh soaring on high.

He lends aid to the slaves of the friends of God,

And advances to high place them who seek him.

Were I to tell his praises till the last day,

My words would not be too many nor admit of
curtailment,

He is the sun of the spirit, not that of the sky,

For from his light men and angels draw life.

That sun is hidden in the form of a man,

Understand me! Allah knows the truth.

O 'Ali, out of all forms of religious service

Choose thou the shadow of that dear friend of God!

Every man takes refuge in some form of service,

And chooses for himself some asylum;

Do thou seek refuge in the shadow of the wise man,

That thou mayest escape thy fierce secret foes.

Of all forms of service this is the fittest for thee;

Thou shalt surpass all who were before thee.

Having chosen thy Director, be submissive to him,

Even as Moses submitted to the commands of Khizr.[2]

Have patience with Khizr's actions, O sincere one!

Lest he say, 'There is a partition between us.'

Though he stave in thy boat, yet hold thy peace;

Though he slay a young man, heave not a sigh.

God declares his hand to be even as God's hand,

For He saith, 'The hand of God is over their hands.'[3]

The hand of God impels him and gives him life;

Nay, not life only, but an eternal soul.

A friend is needed; travel not the road alone,

Take not thy own way through this desert!

Whoso travels this road alone

Only does so by aid of the might of holy men.

The hand of the Director is not weaker than theirs;

His hand is none other than the grasp of Allah!

If absent saints can confer such protection,

Doubtless present saints are more powerful than absent.

If such food be bestowed on the absent,

What dainties may not the guest who is present expect?

The courtier who attends in the presence of the king

Is served better than the stranger outside the gate.

The difference between them is beyond calculation;

One sees the light, the other only the veil.

Strive to obtain entrance within,

If thou wouldst not remain as a ring outside the
    door.

Having chosen thy Director, be not weak of heart,

Nor yet sluggish and lax as water and mud;

But if thou takest umbrage at every rub,

How wilt thou become a polished mirror?"

Notes

1. *I.e.*, the Pir, or Perfect Shaikh, or Spiritual Director. So
   St. John of the Cross and St. Theresa enjoin obedience to
   the Director (Vaughan, xii. 122).
2. See Koran xviii. 77 for the story of Moses and Khizr. It is
   also given in Parnell's 'Hermit.'
3. Koran xlviii. 10.

BOOK II

STORY TWO

THE PAUPER AND
THE PRISONERS (P. 113)

Acertain pauper obtained admittance to a prison, and annoyed the prisoners by eating up all their victuals and leaving them none. At last they made a formal complaint to the Qázi, and prayed him to banish the greedy pauper from the prison. The Qázi summoned the pauper before him, and asked him why he did not go to his own house instead of living on the prisoners. The pauper replied that he had no house or means of livelihood except that supplied by the prison; whereupon the Qázi ordered him to be carried through the city, and proclamation to be made that he was a pauper, that no one might be induced to lend him money or trade with him. Accordingly the attendants sought for a camel whereon to carry him through the city, and at last induced a Kurd who sold firewood to lend his camel for the purpose. The Kurd consented from greed of reward, and the pauper, being seated on the camel, was carried through the city from morning till evening, proclamation being made in Persian, Arabic and Kurdish that he was a pauper. When evening came the Kurd demanded payment, but the pauper refused to give him anything, observing that if he had kept his ears open he must have heard the proclamation. Thus the Kurd was led by greed to spend the day in useless labour.

Satan's office in the world (P. 114)

The pauper said, "Your beneficence is my
   sustenance;
To me, as to aliens, your prison is a paradise.
If you banish me from your prison in reprobation,
I must needs die of poverty and affliction."
Just so Iblis said to Allah, "O have compassion;
Lord! respite me till the day of resurrection.[1]
For in this prison of the world I am at ease,–
That I may slay the children of my enemies.
From every one who has true faith for food,

And as bread for his provisions by the way,

I take it away by fraud or deceit,

So that they raise bitter cries of regret.

Sometimes I menace them with poverty.[2]

Sometimes I blind their eyes with tresses and moles."

In this prison the food of true faith is scarce,

And by the tricks of this dog what there is is lost.

In spite of prayers and fasts and endless pains,

Our food is altogether devoured by him.

Let us seek refuge with Allah from Satan.

Alas! we are perishing by his insolence.

The dog is one, yet he enters a thousand forms;[3]

Whatever he enters straight becomes himself.

Whatever makes you shiver, know he is in it,—

The Devil is hidden beneath its outward form.

When he finds no form at hand, he enters your
   thoughts,

To cause them to draw you into sin.

From your thoughts proceeds destruction,

When from time to time evil thoughts occur to you.

Sometimes thoughts of pleasure, sometimes of
   business,

Sometimes thoughts of science, sometimes of house
and home.

Sometimes thoughts of gain and traffic,

Sometimes thoughts of merchandise and wealth.

Sometimes thoughts of money and wives and
children,

Sometimes thoughts of wisdom or of sadness.

Sometimes thoughts of household goods and fine
linen,

Sometimes thoughts of carpets, sometimes of
sweepers.

Sometimes thoughts of mills, gardens, and villas,

Sometimes of clouds and mists and jokes and jests.

Sometimes thoughts of peace and war,

Sometimes thoughts of honour and disgrace.

Ah! cast out of your head these vain imaginations,

Ah! sweep out of your heart these evil suggestions.

Cry, "There is no power nor strength but in God!"

To avert the Evil One from the world and your own
soul.

*It is the true Beloved who causes all
outward earthly beauty to exist* (P. 115)

Whatsoever is perceived by sense He annuls,

But He stablishes that which is hidden from the
senses.

The lover's love is visible, his Beloved hidden.

The Friend is absent, the distraction he causes
present.

Renounce these affections for outward forms,

Love depends not on outward form or face.

Whatever is beloved is not a mere empty form,

Whether your beloved be of the earth or of heaven.

Whatever be the form you have fallen in love with,—

Why do you forsake it the moment life leaves it?

The form is still there; whence, then, this disgust
at it?

Ah! lover, consider well what is really your beloved.

If a thing perceived by outward senses is the
beloved,

Then all who retain their senses must still love it;

And since love increases constancy,

How can constancy fail while form abides?⁴

But the truth is, the sun's beams strike the wall,

And the wall only reflects that borrowed light.

Why give your heart to mere stones, O simpleton?

Go! seek the source of light which shineth alway!

* * *

Distinguish well true dawn from false dawn,

Distinguish the colour of the wine from that of the cup;

So that, instead of many eyes of caprice,

One eye may be opened through patience and constancy.

Then you will behold true colours instead of false,

And precious jewels in lieu of stones.

But what is a jewel? Nay, you will be an ocean of pearls;

Yea, a sun that measures the heavens!

The real Workman is hidden in His workshop,

Go you into that workshop and see Him face to face.

Inasmuch as over that Workman His work spreads a curtain,

You cannot see Him outside His work.

Since His workshop is the abode of the Wise One,

Whoso seeks Him without is ignorant of Him.

Come, then, into His workshop, which is Not-being,[5]

That you may see the Creator and creation at once.

Whoso has seen how bright is the workshop

Sees how obscure is the outside of that shop.

Rebellious Pharaoh set his face towards Being
    (egoism),

And was perforce blind to that workshop.

Perforce he looked for the Divine decree to change,

And hoped to turn his destiny from his door.

While destiny at the impotence of that crafty one

All the while was secretly mocking.

He slew a hundred thousand guiltless babes

That the ordinance and decree of Allah might be
    thwarted.

That the prophet Moses might not be born alive,

He committed a thousand murders in the land.

He did all this, yet Moses was born,

And was protected against his wrath.

Had he but seen the Eternal workshop,

He had refrained hand and foot from these vain
    devices.

Within his house was Moses safe and sound,
While he was killing the babes outside to no
   purpose.
Just so the slave of lusts who pampers his body
Fancies that some other man bears him ill-will;
Saying this one is my enemy, and this one my foe,
While it is his own body which is his enemy and
   foe,
He is like Pharaoh, and his body is like Moses,
He runs abroad crying, "Where is my foe?"
While lust is in his house, which is his body,
He bites his finger in spite against strangers.

Then follows an anecdote of a man who slew his
mother because she was always misconducting herself
with strangers, and who excused himself by pleading
that if he had not done so he would have been obliged
to slay strangers every day, and thus incur blood-
guiltiness. Lust is likened to this abandoned mother;
when it is once slain, you are at peace with all men. In
answer to an objection that if this were so the prophets
and saints, who have subdued lust, would not have been
hated and oppressed as they were, it is pointed out that

they who hated the prophets in reality hated themselves, just as sick men quarrel with the physician or boys with the teacher. Prophets and saints are created to test the dispositions of men, that the good may be severed from the bad. The numerous grades of prophets, of saints, and of holy men are ordained, as so many curtains of the light of God, to tone down its brilliance, and make it visible to all grades of human sight.

Notes

1. Koran vii. 13.
2. Koran ii. 279.
3. Cf. Gulshan i Raz, p. 86.
4. This couplet exercises both the Turkish and the Lucknow commentators.
5. *I.e.*, annihilation of self and of all phenomenal being, regarding self as naught in the presence of the Deity.

THE FALCON AND
THE OWLS <small>(P. 125)</small>

A certain falcon lost his way, and found himself in the waste places inhabited by owls. The owls suspected that he had come to seize their nests, and all surrounded him to make an end of him. The falcon assured them that he had no such design as they imputed to him, that his abode was on the wrist of the king, and that he did not envy their foul habitation. The owls replied that he was trying to deceive them, inasmuch as such a strange bird as he could not be a favourite of the king. The falcon repeated that he was indeed a favourite of the king, and that the king would assuredly destroy their houses if they injured him, and proceeded to give them some good advice on the folly of trusting to outward appearances. He said, "It is true I am not homogeneous with the king, but yet the king's light is reflected in me, as water becomes homogeneous with earth in plants. I am, as it were, the dust beneath the king's feet; and if you become like me in this respect, you will be exalted as I am. Copy the outward form you behold in me, and perchance you will reach the real substance of the king."

The right use of forms (p. 126)

That my outward form may not mislead you,
Digest my sweet advice before copying me.
Many are they who have been captured by form,
Who aimed at form, and found Allah.
After all, soul is linked to body,
Though it in nowise resembles the body.
The power of the light of the eye is mated with fat,
The light of the heart is hidden in a drop of blood.
Joy harbours in the kidneys and pain in the liver,
The lamp of reason in the brains of the head;
Smell in the nostrils and speech in the tongue,
Concupiscence in the flesh and courage in the heart.

These connections are not without a why and a how,

But reason is at a loss to understand the how.

Universal Soul had connection with Partial Soul,[1]

Which thence conceived a pearl and retained it in its
    bosom.

From that connection, like Mary.

Soul became pregnant of a fair Messiah;—

Not that Messiah who walked upon earth and
    water,

But that Messiah who is higher than space.[2]

Next, as Soul became pregnant by the Soul of
    souls,

So by the former Soul did the world become
    pregnant;

Then the World brought forth another world,

And of this last are brought forth other worlds.

Should I reckon them in my speech till the last day

I should fail to tell the total of these resurrections.[3]

Notes

1. This is a figurative account of the emanations of Absolute Being, whereby the world of phenomena is constituted (see Gulshan i Raz, p. 21, note, and p. 66).

2. *I.e.*, the spirit of the Prophet Muhammad, whom the Sufis identify with the Primal Soul.

3. "Continually is creation born again in a new creation" (Gulshan i Raz, p. 66). By constant effluxes from Absolute Being the world of phenomena is every moment renewed.

THE MAN WHO MADE
A PET OF A BEAR (P. 143)[1]

A kind man, seeing a serpent overcoming a bear, went to the bear's assistance, and delivered him from the serpent. The bear was so sensible of the kindness the man had done him that he followed him about wherever he went, and became his faithful slave, guarding him from everything that might annoy him. One day the man was lying asleep, and the bear, according to his custom, was sitting by him and driving off the flies. The flies became so persistent in their annoyances that the bear lost patience, and seizing the largest stone he could find, dashed it at them in order to crush them utterly; but unfortunately the flies escaped, and the stone lighted upon the sleeper's face and crushed it. The moral is, "Do not make friends with fools." In the course of this story occur anecdotes of a blind man, of Moses rebuking the worshippers of the calf, and of the Greek physician Galen and a madman.

He who needs mercy finds it (P. 143)

Doing kindness is the game and quarry of good men,
A good man seeks in the world only pains to cure.
Wherever there is a pain there goes the remedy,
Wherever there is poverty there goes relief.
Seek not water, only show you are thirsty,
That water may spring up all around you.
That you may hear the words, "The Lord gives them
    to drink,"[2]
Be athirst! Allah knows what is best for you.
Seek you the water of mercy? Be downcast,
And straightway drink the wine of mercy to
    intoxication.
Mercy is called down by mercy to the last.
Withhold not, then, mercy from any one, O son!

* * *

If of yourself you cannot journey to the Ka'ba,
Represent your helplessness to the Reliever.

Cries and groans are a powerful means,

And the All-Merciful is a mighty nurse.

The nurse and the mother keep excusing themselves,

Till their child begins to cry.

In you too has God created infant needs;

When they cry out, their milk is brought to them;

God said, "Call on God;" continue crying,

So that the milk of His love may boil up.[3]

Moses and the worshipper of the calf (P. 145)

Moses said to one of those full of vain imaginations,

"O malevolent one, through error and heresy

You entertain a hundred doubts as to my
    prophethood,

Notwithstanding these proofs, and my holy
    character.

You have seen thousands of miracles done by me,

Yet they only multiply your doubts and cavils.

Through doubts and evil thoughts you are in a
    strait,

You speak despitefully of my prophethood.

I brought the host out of the Red Sea before all men,

That ye might escape the oppression of the
    Egyptians.

For forty years meat and drink came from heaven,

And water sprang from the rock at my prayer.

My staff became a mighty serpent in my hand,

Water became blood for my ill-conditioned enemy.

The staff became a snake, and my hand bright as the
    sun;

From the reflection of that light the sun became a
    star.

Have not these incidents, and hundreds more like
    them,

Banished these doubts from you, O cold-hearted
    one?

The calf lowed through magic,

And you bowed down to it, saying, 'Thou art my
    God.'[4]

*   *   *

The golden calf lowed; but what did it say,

That the fools should feel all this devotion to it?

You have seen many more wondrous works done
   by me,

But where is the base man who accepts the truth?

What is it that charms vain men but vanity?

What else pleases the foolish but folly?

Because each kind is charmed by its own kind,

Does a cow ever seek the lion?

Did the wolf show love to Joseph,[5]

Or only fraud upon fraud with a view to devour
   him?

True, if it lose his wolf-like nature it becomes a
   friend;

Even as the dog of the cave became a son of man.[6]

When good Abu Bakr saw Muhammad,

He recognised his truth, saying, 'This one is true;'

When Abu Bakr caught the perfume of Muhammad,

He said, 'This is no false one.'

But Abu Jahl, who was not one of the sympathisers,

Saw the moon split asunder, yet believed not.

If from a sympathiser, to whom it is well known,

I withhold the truth, still 'tis not hidden from him;

But he who is ignorant and without sympathy,

However much I show him the truth, he sees it not.
The mirror of the heart must needs be polished
Before you can distinguish fair and foul therein."

Notes

1. Anwari Suhaili, i. 27.
2. Koran lxxvi. 21.
3. Koran xvii. 110.
4. See Koran xx. 90.
5. Koran xii. 17.
6. Koran xviii. 17.

STORY TEN

BÁYAZÍD AND
THE SAINT (P. 149)

The celebrated Sufi, Abu Yazíd or Báyazíd of
Bastám, in Khorasan, who lived in the third
century of the Flight, was once making a pilgrimage to
Mecca, and visiting all the "Pillars of insight" who lived
in the various towns that lay on his route. At last he
discovered the "Khizr of the age" in the person of a
venerable Darvesh, with whom he held the following
conversation:—

The Sage said, "Whither are you going, O Báyazíd?
Where will you bring your caravan to a halt?"
Báyazíd replied, "At dawn I start for the Ka'ba."
Quoth the Sage, "What provision for the way have
    you?"
He answered, "I have two hundred silver dirhams;

See them tied up tightly in the corner of my cloak."

The Sage said, "Circumambulate me seven times;

Count this better than circumambulating the Ka'ba;

And as for the dirhams, give them to me, O liberal
one,

And know you have finished your course and
obtained your wish,

You have made the pilgrimage and gained the life to
come,

You have become pure, and that in a moment of
time.

Of a truth that is God which your soul sees in me,

For God has chosen me to be His house.

Though the Ka'ba is the house of His grace and
favours,

Yet my body too is the house of His secret.

Since He made *that* house He has never entered it,

But none but That Living One enters *this* house.[1]

When you have seen me you have seen God,

And have circumambulated the veritable Ka'ba.

To serve me is to worship and praise God;

Think not that God is distinct from me.

Open clear eyes and look upon me,

That you may behold the light of God in a mortal.
The Beloved once called the Ka'ba 'My house,'
But has said to me 'O my servant' seventy times.
O Báyazíd, you have found the Ka'ba,
You have found a hundred precious blessings."
Báyazíd gave heed to these deep sayings,
And placed them as golden earrings in his ears.

Then follow anecdotes of the Prophet paying a visit
to one of his disciples who lay sick, of Shaikh Bahlol,
nicknamed "The Madman," who was a favourite at the
court of Harunu-'r-Rashid, and of the people of Moses.

The sweet uses of adversity (p. 150)

The sick man said, "Sickness has brought me this
   boon,
That this Prince (Muhammad) has come to me this
   morn,
So that health and strength may return to me
From the visit of this unparalleled King.
O blessed pain and sickness and fever!

O welcome weariness and sleeplessness by night!

Lo! God of His bounty and favour

Has sent me this pain and sickness in my old age;

He has given me pain in the back, that I may not
fail

To spring up out of my sleep at midnight;

That I may not sleep all night like the cattle,

God in His mercy has sent me these pains,

At my broken state the pity of kings has boiled up,

And hell is put to silence by their threats!"

Pain is a treasure, for it contains mercies;

The kernel is soft when the rind is scraped off.

O brother, the place of darkness and cold

Is the fountain of life and the cup of ecstasy.

So also is endurance of pain and sickness and
disease.

For from abasement proceeds exaltation.

The spring seasons are hidden in the autumns,

And autumns are charged with springs; flee them
not.

Consort with grief and put up with sadness,

Seek long life in your own death!

Since 'tis bad, whatever lust says on this matter
Heed it not, its business is opposition.
But act contrary thereto, for the prophets
Have laid this injunction upon the world.[2]
Though it is right to take counsel in affairs,
That you may have less to regret in the upshot;—
The prophets have laboured much
To make the world revolve on this pivot stone;[3]
But, in order to destroy the people, lust desires
To make them go astray and lose their heads;—
The people say, 'With whom shall we take counsel?'
The prophets answer, 'With the reason of your chief.'
Again they say, 'Suppose a child or a woman enter,
Who lacks reason and clear judgement;'
They reply, 'Take counsel with them,
And act contrary to what they advise.'
Know your lust to be woman, and worse than woman;
Woman is partial evil, lust universal evil.
If you take counsel with your lust,
See you act contrary to what that base one advises.

Even though it enjoin prayers and fasting,
It is treacherously laying a snare for you.'

*　*　*

You must abandon and ignore your own knowledge,
And dip your hand in the dish of abnegation of
　knowledge.
Whatever seems profitable, flee from it,
Drink poison and spill the water of life.
Contemn whatever praises you,
Lend to paupers your wealth and profits!
Quit your sect and be a subject of aversion,
Cast away name and fame and seek disgrace!"

God the Author of good and evil (P. 156)

If you seek the explanation of God's love and favour,
In connection therewith read the chapter
　"Brightness."4
And if you say evil also proceeds from Him,
Yet what damage is that to His perfection?
To send that evil is one of His perfections.
I will give you an illustration, O arrogant one;

The heavenly Artist paints His pictures of two sorts,
Fair pictures and pictures the reverse of fair.
Joseph he painted fair and made him beautiful;
He also painted ugly pictures of demons and *'afrits*.
Both sorts of pictures are of His workmanship,
They proceed not from His imperfection, but His
    skill,
That the perfection of His wisdom may be shown,
And the gainsayers of His art be put to shame.
Could He not paint ugly things He would lack art,
And therefore He creates Guebers as well as
    Moslems.
Thus, both infidelity and faith bear witness to Him,
Both alike bow down before His almighty sway,
But know, the faithful worship Him willingly,
For they seek and aim at pleasing Him;
While Guebers worship Him unwillingly,
Their real aim and purpose being quite otherwise.

Evil itself is turned into good for the good (p. 157)

The Prophet said to that sick man,
"Pray in this wise and allay your difficulties;
'Give us good in the house of our present world,
And give us good in the house of our next world.[5]
Make our path pleasant as a garden,
And be Thou, O Holy One, our goal!'"
The faithful will say on the last day, "O King!
Was not Hell on the route all of us travelled?
Did not faithful as well as infidels pass through it?
Yet on our way we perceived not the smoke of the
      fire;
Nay, it seemed Paradise and the mansion of the
      blessed."
Then the King will answer, "That green garden,
As it appeared to you on your passage through it,
Was indeed Hell and the place of dread torment;
Yet for you it became a garden green with trees.
Since you have laboured to make hellish lusts,
And the fire of pride that courts destruction,–

To make these, I say, pure and clean,—
And, to please God, have quenched those fires,
So that the fire of lust, that erst breathed flame,
Has become a holy garden and a guiding light,—
Since you have turned the fire of wrath to meekness,
And the darkness of ignorance to shining
  knowledge,
Since you have turned the fire of greed into bounty,
And the vile thorns of malice into a rose-garden;
Since you have quenched all these fires of your own
For my sake, so that those poisons are now pure
  sweets;—
Since you have made fiery lust as a verdant garden,
And have sowed therein the seed of fidelity,
So that nightingales of prayer and praise
Ever warble sweetly around this garden;—
Since you have responded to the call of God,
And have drawn water out of the hell of lust,—
For this cause my hell also, for your behoof,
Becomes a verdant garden and yields leaves and
  fruit."
What is the recompense of well-doing, O son?

It is kindness and good treatment and rich requital.

Have ye not said, "We are victims,

Mere nothings before eternal Being?

If we are drunkards or madmen,

'Tis *that* Cup-bearer and *that* Cup which made us so.

We bow down our heads before His edict and
   ordinance,

We stake precious life to gain His favour.

While the thought of the Beloved fills out hearts,

All our work is to do Him service and spend life for
   Him.

Wherever He kindles His destructive torch,

Myriads of lovers' souls are burnt therewith,

The lovers who dwell within the sanctuary

Are moths burnt with the torch of the Beloved's
   face."

O heart haste thither,[6] for God will shine upon you,

And seem to you a sweet garden instead of a terror.

He will infuse into your soul a new soul,

So as to fill you, like a goblet, with wine.

Take up your abode in His soul!

Take up your abode in heaven, O bright full moon!

Like the heavenly Scribe,[7] He will open your heart's
book

That He may reveal mysteries unto you.

Abide with your Friend, since you have gone astray,

Strive to be a full moon; you are now a fragment
thereof.

Wherefore this shrinking of the part from its
whole?

Why this association with its foes?

Behold Genus become Species in due course,

Behold secrets become manifest through his light!

So long as woman-like you swallow blandishments,

How, O wise man, can you get relief from false
flatteries?

These flatteries and fair words and deceits (of lust)

You take, and swallow, just like women.

But the reproaches and the blows of Darveshes

Are really better for you than the praises of sinners.

Take the light blows of Darveshes, not the honey of
sinners,

And become, by the fortune of good, good yourself.

Because from them the robe of good fortune is
    gained,

In the asylum of the spirit blood becomes life.

Notes

1. Alluding to the *Hadis*: "Heaven and earth contain me not,
   but the heart of my faithful servant contains me."
2. Freytag quotes a saying of 'Omar, "A fool may indicate the
   right course" (Arabum Proverbia, i. p. 566).
3. The law defining the right course.
4. Koran xciii.: "By the noonday brightness, and by the night
   when it darkeneth, thy Lord hath not forsaken thee nor
   been displeased."
5. "O Lord, give us good in this world and good in the next,
   and save us from the torment of the fire." (Koran ii, 197).
6. *I.e.*, to annihilation of self in God, as a moth in the flame.
7. Atarid or Mercury.

BOOK III

STORY ONE

THE TRAVELLERS
WHO ATE THE
YOUNG ELEPHANT (P. 190)

A party of travellers lost their way in a wilderness, and were well nigh famished with hunger. While they were considering what to do, a sage came up and condoled with them on their unfortunate plight. He told them that there were many young elephants in the adjacent woods, one of which would furnish them an ample meal, but at the same time he warned them that if they killed one, its parents would in all probability track them out and be revenged on them for killing their offspring. Shortly after the travellers saw a plump young elephant, and could not resist killing and eating it. One alone refrained. Then they lay down to rest; but no sooner were they fast asleep than a huge elephant made his appearance and proceeded to smell the breath of each one of the sleepers in turn. Those whom he perceived to have eaten of the young elephant's flesh he slew without mercy, sparing only the one who had been prudent enough to abstain.

God's care for His children (P. 190)

O son, the pious are God's children,

Absent or present He is informed of their state.

Deem Him not absent when they are endangered,

For He is jealous for their lives.

He saith, "These saints are my children,

Though remote and alone and away from their Lord.

For their trial they are orphans and wretched,

Yet in love I am ever holding communion with them.

Thou art backed by all my protection,

My children are, as it were, parts of me.

Verily these Darveshes of mine

Are thousands on thousands, and yet no more than One;

For if not, how did Moses with one magic staff

Turn the realm of Pharaoh upside down?
And if it were not so, how did Noah with one curse
Make East and West alike drowned in his flood?
Nor could one prayer of eloquent Lot
Have razed their strong city against their will,—
Their mighty city, like to Paradise,
Became as a Tigris of black water; go, see its vestige!
Towards Syria is this vestige and memorial,
Thou seest it in passing on the way to Jerusalem.
Thousands of God-fearing prophets
In every age hold divine chastisements in hand.
Should I tell of them my limits would be exceeded,
And not hearts only but very hills would bleed."

Evil deeds give men's prayers
an ill savour in God's nostrils (P. 192)

Thou art asleep, and the smell of that forbidden fruit
Ascends to the azure skies,—
Ascends along with thy foul breath,
Till it overpowers heaven with stench;—

Stench of pride, stench of lust, stench of greed.

All these stink like onions when a man speaks.

Though thou swearest, saying, "When have I eaten?

Have I not abstained from onions and garlic?"

The very breath of that oath tells tales,

As it strikes the nostrils of them that sit with thee.

So too prayers are made invalid by such stenches,[1]

That crooked heart is betrayed by its speech.

The answer to that prayer is, "Be ye driven into
    hell,"[2]

The staff of repulsion is the reward of all deceit.

But, if thy speech be crooked and thy meaning
    straight,

Thy crookedness of words will be accepted of God.

That faithful Bilál, when he called to prayer,

Would devoutly cry, "Come hither, come hither!"

At last men said, "O Prophet, this call is not right,

This is wrong; now, what is thy intention?

O Prophet, and O ambassador of the Almighty,

Provide another Mu'azzin of better talent,

'Tis an error at the beginning of our divine worship

To utter the words, 'Come to the asylum!'"[3]

The wrath of the Prophet boiled up, and he said

(Uttering one or two secrets from the fount of grace),

"O base ones, in God's sight the 'Ho!' of Bilál

Is better than a hundred 'Come hithers' and
   ejaculations.

Ah! excite not a tumult, lest I tell forth openly

Your secret thoughts from first to last.

If ye keep not your breath sweet in prayer,

Go, desire a prayer from the Brethren of Purity!"

For this cause spake God to Moses,

At the time he was asking aid in prayer,

"O Moses! desire protection of me

With a mouth that thou hast not sinned withal."

Moses answered, "I possess not such a mouth."

God said, "Call upon me with another mouth!

Act so that all thy mouths

By night and by day may be raising prayers.

When thou hast sinned with one mouth,

With thy other mouth cry, 'O Allah!'

Or else cleanse thy own mouth,

And make thy spirit alert and quick.

Calling on God is pure, and when purity approaches,

Impurity arises and takes its departure.
Contraries flee away from contraries;
When day dawns night takes flight.
When the pure name (of God) enters the mouth,
Neither does impurity nor that impure mouth
    remain!"

The man whose calling "O Allah" was equivalent
to God's answering him,
"Here am I"[4] (P. 192)

That person one night was crying, "O Allah!"
That his mouth might be sweetened thereby,
And Satan said to him, "Be quiet, O austere one!
How long wilt thou babble, O man of many words?
No answer comes to thee from nigh the throne,
How long wilt thou cry 'Allah' with harsh face?"
That person was sad at heart and hung his head,
And then beheld Khizr present before him in a
    vision,
Who said to him, "Ah! thou hast ceased to call on
    God,

Wherefore repentest thou of calling upon Him?"

The man said, "The answer 'Here am I' came not,

Wherefore I fear that I am repulsed from the door."

Khizr replied to him, "God has given me this
   command;

Go to him and say, 'O much-tried one,

Did not I engage thee to do my service?

Did not I engage thee to call upon me?

That calling 'Allah' of thine *was* my 'Here am I,'

And that pain and longing and ardour of thine my
   messenger;

Thy struggles and strivings for assistance

Were my attractions, and originated thy prayer.

Thy fear and thy love are the covert of my mercy,

Each 'O Lord!' of thine contains many 'Here am I's.'"

The soul of fools is alien from this calling on God,

Because it is not their wont to cry, 'O Lord!'

On their mouths and hearts are locks and bonds,[5]

That they may not cry to God in time of distress.

God gave Pharaoh abundance of riches and wealth,

So that he boasted that he was 'Lord Supreme.'

In the whole of his life he suffered no headache,

So that he never cried to God, wretch that he was.

God granted him the absolute dominion of the
world,

But withheld from him pain and sorrow and cares;

Because pain and sorrow and loads of cares

Are the lot of God's friends in the world.

Pain is better than the dominion of the world,

So that thou mayest call on God in secret.

The cries of those free from pain are dull and cold,

The cries of the sorrowful come from the burning
hearts."

Notes

1. "Whoever eats garlic or onions must keep away from me or
from the *Masjid*" (Mishkát ul Másábih, ii. 321).
2. Koran xxiii. 110 : "He will say, 'Be ye driven down into it,
and address me not.'
3. Rules for the call to prayer are given in Mishkát ul Másábih,
i. 141.
4. Or, "What dost thou require of me?"
5. Koran ii. 6.

THE JACKAL WHO PRETENDED TO BE A PEACOCK _(P. 204)

A jackal fell into a dye-pit, and his skin was dyed of various colours. Proud of his splendid appearance, he returned to his companions, and desired them to address him as a peacock. But they proceeded to test his pretensions, saying, "Dost thou scream like a peacock, or strut about gardens as peacocks are wont to do?" And he was forced to admit that he did not, whereupon they rejected his pretensions. Another story, also on the subject of false pretenders, follows. A proud man who lacked food procured a skin full of fat, greased his beard and lips with it, and called on his friends to observe how luxuriously he had dined. But his belly was vexed at this, because it was hungry, and he was destroying his chance of being invited to dinner by his friends. So the belly cried to God, and a cat came and carried off the skin of fat, and so the man's false pretences were exposed. The poet takes occasion to point out that Pharaoh's pretensions to divinity exactly resembled the pretensions of this jackal, and adds that all such false pretenders may be detected by the mark noted in the Koran, "Ye shall know them by the strangeness of their speech."[1] This recalls the story of Harut and Marut, two angels who were very severe on the frailties of mankind, and whom God sent down upon the earth to be tempted, with the result that they both succumbed to the charms of the daughters of men.[2]

Notes

1. Koran xlvii. 32.
2. Koran ii. 96.

THE ELEPHANT IN A
DARK ROOM (P. 217)

S ome Hindoos were exhibiting an elephant in a dark
room, and many people collected to see it. But as
the place was too dark to permit them to see the
elephant, they all felt it with their hands, to gain an idea
of what it was like. One felt its trunk, and declared that
the beast resembled a water-pipe; another felt its ear,
and said it must be a large fan; another its leg, and
thought it must be a pillar; another felt its back, and
declared the beast must be like a great throne.
According to the part which each felt, he gave a
different description of the animal. One, as it were, called
it "*Dal,*" and another "*Alif.*"

Comparison of the sensual eye to the
hand of one that felt the elephant (P. 217)

The eye of outward sense is as the palm of a hand,
The whole of the object is not grasped in the palm.
The sea itself is one thing, the foam another;
Neglect the foam, and regard the sea with your eyes.
Waves of foam rise from the sea night and day,
You look at the foam ripples and not the mighty sea.
We, like boats, are tossed hither and thither,
We are blind though we are on the bright ocean.
Ah! you who are asleep in the boat of the body,
You see the water; behold the Water of waters!
Under the water you see there is another Water
    moving it,
Within the spirit is a Spirit that calls it.
Where were Moses and Jesus when that Sun
Showered down water on the fields sown with corn?
Where were Adam and Eve that time
God Almighty fitted the string to His bow?
The one form of speech is evil and defective;
The other form, which is not defective, is perfect.

If I speak thereof your feet stumble,

Yet if I speak not of it, woe be to you!

And if I speak in terms of outward form,

You stick fast in that same form, O son.

You are footbound like the grass in the ground,

And your head is shaken by the wind uncertainly,

Your foot stands not firmly till you move it,

Nay, till you pluck it not up from the mire.

When you pluck up your foot you escape from the
   mire,

The way to this salvation is very difficult.

When you obtain salvation at God's hands,
   O wanderer,

You are free from the mire, and go your way.

When the suckling is weaned from its nurse,

It eats strong meats and leaves the nurse.

You are bound to the bosom of earth like seeds,

Strive to be weaned through nutriment of the heart.

Eat the words of wisdom, for veiled light

Is not accepted in preference to unveiled light.

When you have accepted the light, O beloved,

When you behold what is veiled without a veil,

Like a star you will walk upon the heavens;
Nay, though not in heaven, you will walk on high.

*   *   *

Keep silence, that you may hear Him speaking
Words unutterable by tongue in speech.
Keep silence, that you may hear from that Sun
Things inexpressible in books and discourses.
Keep silence, that the Spirit may speak to you;
Give up swimming and enter the ark of Noah;
Not like Canaan when he was swimming,
Who said, "I desire not to enter the ark of Noah
  passing by."

Noah and his unbelieving son Canaan (p. 218)

Noah cried, "Ho! child, come into the ark and rest,
That you be not drowned in the flood, O weak
  one."[1]
Canaan said, "Nay! I have learned to swim,
I have lit a torch of my own apart from thy torch."
Noah replied, "Make not light of it, for 'tis the flood
  of destruction,

Swimming with hands and feet avails naught
    to-day.

The wind of wrath and the storm blow out torches;

Except the torch of God, all are extinguished."

He answered, "Nay! I am going to that high
    mountain,

For that will save me from all harm."

Noah cried, "Beware, do not so, mountains are now
    as grass;

Except the Friend none can save thee."

He answered, "Why should I listen to thy advice?

For thou desirest to make me one of thy flock.

Thy speech is by no means pleasing to me,

I am free from thee in this world and the next."

* * *

Thus the more good advice Noah gave him,

The more stubborn refusals he returned.

Neither was his father tired of advising Canaan,

Nor did his advice make any impression on Canaan;

While they were yet talking a violent wave

Smote Canaan's head, and he was overwhelmed.

Reconciliation of the two traditions,
"Acquiescence in infidelity is infidelity," and
"Whoso acquiesces not in God's ordinance desires
another Lord besides me" (P. 219)

Yesterday an inquirer questioned me,
Since he was interested in the foregoing narrative,
Saying, "The Prophet, whose words are as a seal,
Said, 'Acquiescence in infidelity is infidelity.'
And again, 'Acquiescence in God's ordinance
Is incumbent on all true believers.'
Infidelity and hypocrisy are not ordained of God;
If I acquiesce in them I am at variance with God.
And yet, if I acquiesce not, that again is wrong;
What way of escape is there from this dilemma?"
I said to him, "This infidelity is ordained, not
   ordinance,[2]
Though this infidelity is the work of the
   ordinance.
Therefore distinguish the ordinance from the
   ordained,
That thy difficulty may be at once removed.

I acquiesce in infidelity so far as it is God's
    ordinance,

Not so far as it is our evil and foul passions.

Infidelity *quá* ordinance is not infidelity,

Call not God an infidel. Set not foot in this place.

Infidelity is folly, ordained infidelity wisdom,

How can mercy and vengeance be the same?

Ugliness of the picture is not ugliness of the painter,

Not so, for he erases ugly pictures.

The ability of the painter is shown in this,

That he can paint both ugly and beautiful pictures.

If I should pursue this argument properly,

So that questions and answers should be prolonged,

The unction of the mystery of love would escape me,

The picture of obedience would become another
    picture."

Bewilderment from intense love of God puts an end to all thinking and argument[3] (P. 219)

A certain man whose hair was half grey came in
   haste

To a barber who was a friend of his,

Saying, "Pluck out the white hairs from my beard,

For I have selected a young bride, O my son."

The barber cut off his beard and laid it before him,

Saying, "Do you part them, the task is beyond me."

Questions are white and answers black; do you
   choose,

For the man of faith knows not how to choose.

Thus, one smote Zaid a blow,

And Zaid attacked him for his treachery.

The striker said, "Let me first ask you a question,

Give me an answer to it and then strike me;

I struck your back and a bruise appeared,

Now I ask you a question in all kindliness,

Did this bruise proceed from my hand,

Or from the smitten part of your back,
   O complainer?"

Zaid replied, "Through pain I am not in a condition
To enter upon thought and consideration of this.
You, who are free from pain, think this out;
Such trifling thoughts occur not to a man in pain."
[Men in pain have no time for other thoughts,
Whether you enter mosque or Christian church.
Your carelessness and injustice suggest thoughts
And unprecedented difficulties to your imagination.
The man in pain cares only for the faith,
He is aware only of man and his work.
He sets God's command upon his head and face,
And for thinking, he puts it aside.[4]]

Notes

1. Koran xi. 44.
2. Or "decreed, not decree" (*maqzi nai qaza*). I confess I do not understand the distinction.
3. See Gulshan i Raz, l. 287.
4. The four last couplets are omitted in the Bulaq edition.

STORY TEN

THE OLD MAN
WHO MADE NO
LAMENTATION AT THE
DEATH OF HIS SONS (P. 229)

After short anecdotes of Pharaoh's magicians, of the mule who complained to the camel that he was always stumbling, and of the prophet Ezra, comes the story of the old man who wept not for the death of his sons.

An old man who was noted for sanctity, and who realised the saying of the Prophet, "The 'ulama of the faith are as the prophets of Israel," lost all his sons, but showed no grief or regret. His wife therefore rebuked him for his want of feeling, whereupon he replied to her as follows :—

He turned to his wife and said, "O dame,

The harvest of December is not as that of July;

Though they be dead or though they be living,

Are they not equally visible to the eyes of the heart?

I behold them clearly before me,

Wherefore should I disfigure my countenance like
you?

Though they have gone forth by revolution of
fortune,

They are with me still, playing round me.

The cause of lamentation is separation or parting,

But I am still with my dear ones, and embrace them.

Ordinary people may see them in dreams,

But I see them clearly, though wide awake.

I conceal myself a while from this world,

I shake down the leaves of outward sense from the
tree.

Know, O wife, outward sense is captive to reason,

And reason, again, is captive to spirit.

Spirit unlooses the chained hands of reason;

Yea, it opens all things that are closed.

Sensations and thoughts resemble weeds

Which occupy the surface of pure water.

The hand of reason puts these weeds aside,

And the pure water is then visible to the wise.

Weeds in plenty cover the streams like bubbles;

When they are swept aside, the water is seen;

But when God unlooses not the hands of reason,

The weeds on our water grow thick through carnal
lust;

Yea, they cover up your water more and more,

While your lust is smiling and your reason weeping.

When fear of God binds the hands of lust,

Then God unlooses the two hands of reason.

Then the powerful senses are subdued by you,

When you submit to reason as your commander.

Then your sleepless sense is lulled into sleep,

That mysteries may appear to the soul.

You behold visions when broad awake,

And the gates of heaven are open before you."

BAHLOL AND
THE DARVESH <small>(P. 232)</small>

The foregoing story is followed by anecdotes of a
blind saint who was miraculously enabled to read
the Koran, of Luqman and David, and a description of
the saints who, mindful of the saying, "Patience is the
key of happiness," resign themselves to the dispensa-
tions of Providence, and never pray to have them
altered. The story of Bahlol and the Darvesh is then
given as an example of this resignation to the will of
God. Bahlol once paid a visit to a saintly Darvesh, and
asked him how he fared. The Darvesh replied, "I fare
like a man who directs the course of the world as he
wills, to whom death and life are subservient, and
whom the stars themselves obey." Bahlol then pressed
him to explain his meaning more clearly, and the
Darvesh replied as follows :–

He said, "This at least is notorious to all men,

That the world obeys the command of God.

Not a leaf falls from a tree

Without the decree and command of that Lord of
    lords;

Not a morsel goes from the mouth down the throat

Till God says to it, 'Go down.'

Desire and appetite, which are the reins of mankind,

Are themselves subservient to the rule of God.

             *   *   *

Hear this much, that, whereas the totality of actions

Is not effected without God's direction,

When the decree of God becomes the pleasure of
    man,

Then man desires the fulfilment of God's decrees;

And this too spontaneously, not in hope of reward,

But because his very nature is congruous therewith.

He desires not even his own life for himself,

Nor is he relying on the hope of sweets of life to
    come.

Whatever path is taken by the eternal decree,

Whether it be life or death, 'tis all one to him.

He lives for the sake of God, not for wealth;

He dies for the sake of God, not in fear and grief.

His faith is based on his desire to do God's will,

Not on hope to gain paradise with its groves and
founts.

His avoidance of infidelity is also for God's sake,

It proceeds not from fear of falling into the fire.

Thus this temper of his arises from his very nature,

Not from any discipline and endeavour of his own.

At times he laughs when he contemplates God's
pleasure,

God's decrees are to him as sweetmeats of sugar.

I ask, does not the world march agreeably to the will

And commands of a man rejoicing in this
disposition?

Why, then, should such an one make prayers and
petitions,

Saying, 'O God, change such and such a decree?'

His own death and his children's deaths

For God's sake seem to him as sweets in the mouth.

In the view of that faithful one his children's deaths

Are as sweetmeats to a starving beggar.

Why, therefore, should he make prayers
Unless he pray for what is pleasing to God?
These prayers and petitions, not those of self-pity
Make that man to be endued with salvation.
He utterly burned up all his self-pity,
At the time when he lit the lamp of love to God.
His love was the hell that burned up his inclinations;
Yea, he burned up his own inclinations one by one."

MIRACLES PERFORMED BY THE PROPHET MUHAMMAD (P. 260)

It is related that the Prophet was once present at a banquet, and after he had eaten and drunk, his servant Anas threw the napkin which he had used into the fire, and the napkin was not burnt, but only purified by the fire. On another occasion a caravan of Arabs was travelling in the desert, and was in sore distress through lack of water, whereupon the Prophet miraculously increased the water in a single water-skin, so that it sufficed to supply the needs of all the travellers. Moreover, the negro who carried the water-skin was rendered as white and fair as Joseph. Again, a heathen women came to the Prophet carrying her infant, aged only two months, and the infant saluted the

Prophet as the veritable apostle of God. Again, when the prophet was about to put on his sandals, an eagle swooped down upon one of them and carried it off, when a viper was seen to drop from the sandal. The Prophet was at first inclined to grumble at this stroke of ill-luck; but when he saw the viper his discontent was turned into thankfulness to God, who had thus miraculously saved him from being bitten by the viper.

In difficulties there is provided
a way of salvation[1] (p. 263)

In this tale there is a warning for thee, O soul,
That thou mayest acquiesce in God's ordinances,
And be wary and not doubt God's benevolence,
When sudden misfortunes befall thee.
Let others grow pale from fear of ill fortune,
Do thou smile like the rose at loss and gain;
For the rose, though its petals be torn asunder,
Still smiles on, and it is never cast down.
It says, "Why should I fall into grief in disgrace?
I gather beauty even from the thorn of disgrace."

Whatsoever is lost to thee through God's decree
Know of a surety is so much gained from misfortune.
What is Sufiism? 'Tis to find joy in the heart
Whensoever distress and care assail it.
Know troubles to be that eagle of the Prophet's
Which carried off the sandal of that holy one,
In order to save his foot from the bite of the viper-
O excellent device! – to preserve him from harm.
'Tis said, "Mourn not for your slaughtered cattle
If a wolf has harried your flocks;"
For that calamity may avert a greater calamity,
And that loss may ward off a more grievous loss.

Notes

1. Freytag, Arabum Proverbia, vol. iii. p. 334.

BOOK IV

STORY ONE

THE LOVER AND
HIS MISTRESS (P. 303)

The fourth book begins with an address to Husamu-
'd-Din, and this is followed by the story of the
lover and his mistress, already commenced in the third
book. A certain lover had been separated from his
mistress for the space of seven years, during which he
never relaxed his efforts to find her. At last his
constancy and perseverance were rewarded, in
accordance with the promises "The seeker shall find,"
and "Whoso shall have wrought an atom's weight of
good shall behold it."[1] One night, as he was wandering
through the city, he was pursued by the patrol, and, in
order to escape them, took refuge in a garden, where he
found his long-sought mistress. This occasioned him to
reflect how often men "hate the things that are good for
them,"[2] and led him to bless the rough patrol who had

procured him the bliss of meeting with his mistress. *Apropos* of this, an anecdote is told of a preacher who was in the habit of blessing robbers and oppressors, because their evil example had turned him to righteousness. The moment the lover found himself alone with his mistress, he attempted to embrace her, but his mistress repulsed him, saying, that though no men were present, yet the wind was blowing and that showed that God, the mover of the wind, was also present. The lover replied, "It may be I am lacking in good manners, but I am not lacking in constancy and fidelity towards you." His mistress replied, "One must judge of the hidden by the manifest; I see for myself that your outward behaviour is bad, and thence I cannot but infer that your boast of hidden virtues is not warranted by actual facts. You are ashamed to misconduct yourself in the sight of men, but have no scruple to do so in the presence of the All-seeing God, and hence I doubt the existence of the virtuous sentiments which you claim to possess, but which can only be known to yourself." To illustrate this, she told the story of a Sufi and his faithless wife.

This wife was one day entertaining a paramour, when she was surprised by the sudden return of her husband.

On the spur of the moment she threw a woman's dress over her paramour and presented him to her husband as a rich lady who had come to propose a marriage between her son and the Sufi's daughter, saying she did not care for wealth, but only regarded modesty and rectitude of conduct. To this the Sufi replied, that as from her coming unattended it was plain that the lady had not the wealth she pretended to have, it was more than probable that her pretensions to extraordinary modesty and humility were also fictitious. The lover then proceeded to excuse himself by the plea that he had wished to test his mistress, and ascertain for himself whether she was a modest woman or not. He said he of course knew beforehand that she would prove to be a modest woman, but still he wished to have ocular demonstration of the fact. His mistress reproved him for trying to deceive her with false pretences, assuring him that after he had been detected in a fault, his only proper course was to confess it, as Adam had done. Moreover, she added that an attempt to put her to the test would have been an extremely unworthy proceeding, only to be paralleled by Abu Jahl's attempt to prove the truth of the Prophet's claims by calling on him to perform a miracle.

The soul of good in things evil.
Evil only relative (P. 303)

The lover invoked blessings on that rough patrol,
Because their harshness had wrought bliss for him.
They were poison to most men, but sweets to him,
Because those harsh ones had united him with his
 love.
In the world there is nothing absolutely bad;
Know, moreover, evil is only relative.
In the world there is neither poison nor antidote,
Which is not a foot to one and a fetter to another;
To one the power of moving, to another a clog;
To one a poison, to another an antidote.
Serpents' poison is life to serpents,
In relation to mankind it is death.
To the creatures of the sea the sea is a garden,
To the creatures of the land it is fatal.
In the same way, O man, reckon up with intelligence
The relations of these things in endless variety.
In relation to this man Zaid is as Satan,
In relation to another he is as a Sultan.

The latter calls Zaid a sincere Musulman,

The former calls him a Gueber deserving to be
    killed.

Zaid, one and the same person, is life to the one,

And to the other an annoyance and a pest.

If you desire that God may be pleasing to you,

Then look at Him with the eyes of them that love
    Him.

Look not at that Beauty with your own eyes,

Look at that Object of desire with His votaries' eyes;

Shut your own eyes from beholding that sweet
    Object,

And borrow from His admirers their eyes;

Nay, borrow from Him both eyes and sight,

And with those eyes of His look upon His face,

In order that you may not be disappointed with the
    sight.

God says, "Whoso is God's, God also is his."

God says, "I am his eye, his hand, his heart,"[3]

That his good fortune may emerge from adversity.

Whatsoever is hateful to you, if it should lead you

To your beloved, at once becomes agreeable to you.

Why God is named "Hearing,"
"Seeing," and "Knowing" (P. 307)

God calls himself "Seeing," to the end that

His eye may every moment scare you from sinning.

God calls himself "Hearing," to the end that

You may close your lips against foul discourse.

God calls himself "Knowing," to the end that

You may be afraid to plot evil.

These names are not mere accidental names of God,

As a negro may be called *Kafúr* (white);

They are names derived from God's essential
    attributes,

Not mere vain titles of the First Cause.

For if so, they would be only empty pleasantries,

Like calling the deaf a hearer and the blind a seer,

Or a name like "impudent" for a modest man,

Or "beautiful" for an ugly negro,

Or such a title as *"Háji"* for a new-born boy,

Or that of *"Ghází"* applied to a noble idler.

If such titles as these are used in praising
    persons

Who do not possess the qualities implied, 'tis
  wrong;

'Twould be jesting or mockery or madness.

"God is exalted above" what is said by evil men.[4]

I knew you before I met you face to face,

That you had a fair face but an evil heart;

Yea, I knew you before I saw you,

That you were rooted in iniquity through guile.

When my eye is red owing to inflammation,

I know 'tis so from the pain, though I see it not.

You regarded me as a lamb without a shepherd;

You fancied that I had no guardian.

Lovers have suffered chastisement for this cause,

That they have cast ill-timed looks at fair ones.

They have supposed the fawn to have no shepherd,

They have supposed the captive to be going a
  begging;

Till in the twinkling of an eye an arrow pierces
  them,

Saying, "I am her guardian; look not at her rashly!"

What! am I less than a lamb or a fallow deer,

That I should have none to shepherd me?

Nay, I have a Guardian worthy of dominion,

Who knows every wind that blows upon me.

He is aware whether that wind is chill or mild,

He is not ignorant nor absent, O mean one.

The carnal soul is made by God blind and deaf;

I saw with the heart's eye your blindness afar off.

For this cause I never inquired about you for eight
    years,

Because I saw you filled with ignorance and
    duplicity.

Why indeed should I inquire about one in the
    furnace,

Who is bowed down with reproach, like yourself?

*Comparison of the world to a bath stove,
and of piety to the hot bath* (P. 307)

The lust of the world is like a bath stove,

Whereby the bath of piety is heated;

But the lot of the pious is purity from the stove's
    filth,

Because they dwell in the bath and in cleanliness.

The rich are as those that carry dung
To heat the furnace of the bath withal.
God has instilled into them cupidity,
That the bath may be warmed and pleasant.
Quit this stove and push on into the bath;
Know quitting the stove to be the bath itself.
Whoso is in the stove-room is as a servant
To him who is temperate and prudent.

*   *   *

Your lust is as fire in the world,
With a hundred greedy mouths wide open.
In the judgment of reason this gold is foul dung,
Although, like dung, it serves to kindle the fire.

*   *   *

Whoso was born in the stove-room and never saw
    purity,
The smell of sweet musk is disagreeable to him.

In illustration of this, a story follows of a tanner who was accustomed to bad smells in the course of his trade, and who was half killed by the smell of musk in the bazaar of the perfumers, but was cured by the accustomed smell of dung.

Notes

1. Koran xcix. 7.
2. Koran ii. 213.
3. "My servant draws nigh to me by pious deeds till I love him, and, when I love him, I am his eye, his ear, his tongue, his foot, his hand, and by me he sees, hears, talks, walks, and feels." – *Hadis*.
4. Cp. Koran xvi. 3.

THE YOUTH WHO WROTE A LETTER OF COMPLAINT ABOUT HIS RATIONS TO THE KING (P. 337)

A certain youth in the service of a great king was dissatisfied with his rations, so he went to the cook and reproached him with dishonouring his master by his stinginess. The youth would not listen to his excuses, but wrote off an angry letter of complaint to the king, in terms of outward compliment and respect, but betraying an angry spirit. On receiving this letter, the king observed that it contained only complaints about meat and drink, and evinced no aspirations after spiritual food, and therefore needed no answer, as "the

proper answer to a fool is silence."[1] When the youth
received no answer to his letter, he was much surprised,
and threw the blame on the cook and on the messenger,
ignoring the fact that the folly of his own letter was the
real reason of its being left unanswered. He wrote in all
five letters, but the king persisted in his refusal to reply,
saying that fools are enemies to God and man, and that
he who has any dealings with a fool fouls his own nest.
Fools only regard material meat and drink, whereas the
food of the wise is the light of God, as it is said by the
Prophet, "I pass the night in the presence of my Lord,
who giveth me meat and drink,"[2] and again, "Fasting is
the food of God," *i.e.*, the means by which spiritual food
is obtained.[3]

*Explanation of the text, "And Moses conceived a
secret fear within him. We said 'Fear not, for
thou shalt be uppermost
(over Pharaoh's magicians)'"[4]* (P. 340)

Moses said, "Their sorcery confuses them;
What can I do? These people have no discernment."
God said, "I will generate in them discernment;

[121]

I will make their undiscerning reason to see clearly.

Although like a sea their waves cast up foam,

O Moses, thou shalt prevail over them; fear not!"

The magicians gloried in their own achievements,

But when Moses' rod became a snake, they were
   confounded.

Whoso boasts of his beauty and wit,

The stone of death is a touchstone of his boasts.

Sorcery fades away, but the miracles of Moses
   advance.

Both resemble a dish falling from a roof:

The noise of the dish of sorcery leaves only cursing;

The noise of the dish of faith leaves edification.

When the touchstone is hidden from the sight of all,

Then come forth to battle and boast, O base coin!

Your time for boasting is when the touchstone is
   away;

The hand of power will soon crush your exaltation.

The base coin says to me with pride every moment,

"O pure gold, how am I inferior to you?"

The gold replies, "Even so, O comrade;

But the touchstone is at hand; be ready to meet it!"

Death of the body is a benefaction to the spiritual;

What damage has pure gold to dread from the
shears?

If the base coin were of itself far-sighted,

It would reveal at first the blackness it shows at last.

If it had showed its blackness at first on its face,

'Twould have avoided hypocrisy now and misery at
last.

'Twould have sought the alchemy of grace in due
time;

Its reason would have prevailed over its hypocrisy.

If it became broken-hearted through its own bad
state,

'Twould look onward to Him that heals the broken;

'Twould look to the result and be broken-hearted,

And be made whole at once by the Healer of broken
hearts.

Divine grace places base copper in the alembic,

Adulterated gold is excluded from that favour.

O adulterated gold, boast not, but see clearly

That thy Purchaser is not blind to thy defects.

The light of the judgment-day will enlighten his
eyes

And destroy the glamour of thy fascinations.

Behold them that have regard to the ultimate result,

And also the regrets of foolish souls and their envy.

Behold them that regard only the present,

And cast away thoughts of evil to come from their
minds.

Notes

1. See Freytag, Arabum Proverbia, i. 551, for a parallel.
2. Koran xxvi. 79.
3. See Mishkat ul Masabih, vol. i. p. 463.
4. Koran xx. 70.

BOOK V

STORY ONE

THE PROPHET AND
HIS INFIDEL GUEST (P. 393)

After the usual address to Husamu-'d-Din follows a comment on the precept addressed to Abraham, "Take four birds and draw them towards thee, and cut them in pieces."[1] The birds are explained to be the duck of gluttony, the cock of concupiscence, the peacock of ambition and ostentation, and the crow of bad desires, and this is made the text of several stories. Beginning with gluttony, the poet tells the following story to illustrate the occasion of the Prophet's uttering the saying, "Infidels eat with seven bellies, but the faithful with one." One day some infidels begged food and lodging of the Prophet. The Prophet was moved by their entreaties, and desired each of his disciples to take one of the infidels to his house and feed and lodge him, remarking that it was their duty to show kindness to strangers at his command, as much as to do battle with his foes. So each disciple selected one of the infidels and carried him off to his house; but there was one big and coarse man, a very giant Og, whom no one would receive, and the Prophet took him to his own house. In his house the Prophet had seven she-goats to supply his family with milk, and the hungry infidel devoured all the milk of those seven goats, to say nothing of bread and other viands. He left not a drop for the Prophet's family, who were therefore much annoyed with him, and when he retired to his chamber one of the servant-maids locked him in. During the night the infidel felt very unwell in consequence of having overeaten himself, and tried to get out into the open air, but was unable to do so, owing to the door being locked. Finally, he was very sick, and defiled his bedding. In the morning he was extremely ashamed, and the moment the door was opened he ran away. The Prophet was aware of what had happened, but let the man escape, so as not to put him to shame. After he had gone the servants saw the mess he had made, and informed the Prophet of it; but the Prophet made light of it, and said he would clean it up himself. His friends were shocked at the thought of the Prophet soiling his sacred hands with such filth, and tried to prevent him, but he persisted in doing it, calling to mind the text, "As thou livest, O Muhammad, they were bewildered by drunkenness,"[2] and being, in fact, urged to it by a divine command. While he was engaged in the work the infidel came back to look for a talisman which he had left behind him in his hurry to escape, and seeing the Prophet's occupation he burst into tears, and bewailed his own filthy conduct. The Prophet consoled him, saying that weeping and penitence would purge the offence, for God says, "Little let them laugh, and much let them weep;"[3] and again, "Lend God a liberal loan;"[4] and again, "God only desireth to put away filthiness from you as His household, and with cleansing to cleanse you."[5] The Prophet then urged him to bear witness that God was the Lord, even as was done by the sons of Adam,[6] and explained how the outward acts of prayer and fasting bear witness of the spiritual light within. After being nurtured on this spiritual food the infidel confessed the truth of Islam, and renounced his infidelity and gluttony. He returned thanks to the Prophet for bringing him to the knowledge of the true faith and regenerating him, even as 'Isa had regenerated Lazarus. The Prophet was satisfied of his sincerity, and asked him to sup with him again. At supper he drank only half the portion of milk yielded by one goat, and steadfastly refused to take more, saying he felt perfectly satisfied with the little he had already taken. The other guests marvelled much to see his gluttony so soon cured, and were led to reflect on the virtues of the spiritual food administered to him by the Prophet.

Outward acts bear witness of the state
of the heart within (p. 396)

Prayer and fasting and pilgrimage and holy war
Bear witness of the faith of the heart.
Giving alms and offerings and quitting avarice
Also bear witness of the secret thoughts.
So, a table spread for guests serves as a plain sign,
Saying, "O guest, I am your sincere well-wisher."
So, offerings and presents and oblations
Bear witness, saying, "I am well pleased with you."
Each of these men lavishes his wealth or pains,—
What means it but to say, "I have a virtue within
    me,

Yea, a virtue of piety or liberality,

Whereof my oblations and fasting bear witness"?

Fasting proclaims that he abstains from lawful food,

And that therefore he doubtless avoids unlawful
food.

And his alms say, "He gives away his own goods;

It is therefore plain that he does not rob others."

If he acts thus from fraud, his two witnesses

(Fasting and alms) are rejected in God's court;–

If the hunter scatters grain

Not out of mercy, but to catch game;–

If the cat keeps fast, and remains still

In fasting only to entrap unwary birds;–

Making hundreds of people suspicious,

And giving a bad name to men who fast and are
liberal;–

Yet the grace of God, despite this fraud,

May ultimately purge him from all this hypocrisy.

Mercy may prevail over vengeance, and give the
hypocrite

Such light as is not possessed by the full moon.

God may purge his dealings from that hypocrisy,

And in mercy wash him clean of that defilement.

In order that the pardoning grace of God may be seen,

God pardons all sins that need pardon.

Wherefore God rains down water from the sign Pisces,

To purify the impure from their impurities.[7]

* * *

Thus acts and words are witnesses of the mind within,

From these two deduce inferences as to the thoughts.

When your vision cannot penetrate within,

Inspect the water voided by the sick man.

Acts and words resemble the sick man's water,

Which serves as evidence to the physician of the body.

But the physician of the spirit penetrates the soul,

And thence ascertains the man's faith.

Such an one needs not the evidence of fair acts and words;

"Beware of such, they spy out the heart."

Require this evidence of act and word only from one

Who is not joined to the divine Ocean like a stream.

But the light of the traveller arrived at the goal,

Verily that light fills deserts and wastes.

That witness of his is exempt from bearing witness,

And from all trouble and risk and good works.

Since the brilliance of that jewel beams forth,

It is exempted from these obligations.

Wherefore require not from him act and word
    evidence,

Because both worlds through him bloom like roses.

What is this evidence but manifestation of hidden
    things,

Whether it be evidence in word, or deed, or
    otherwise?

Accidents serve only to manifest the secret essence;

The essential quality abides, and accidents pass
    away.

This mark of gold endures not the touchstone,

But only the gold itself, genuine and undoubted.

These prayers and holy war and fasting

Will not endure, only the noble soul endures.

The soul exhibits acts and words of this sort,

Then it rubs its substance on the touchstone of
    God's command,

Saying, "My faith is true, behold my witnesses!"

But witnesses are open to suspicion.

Know that witnesses must be purified,

And their purification is sincerity, on that you may
    depend.

The witness of word consists in speaking the truth,

The witness of acts in keeping one's promises.

If the witness of word lie, its evidence is rejected,

And if the witness of act play false, it is rejected.

Your words and acts must be without self-
    contradiction

In order to be accepted without question.

"Your aims are different,"[8] and you contradict
    yourselves,

You sew by day, and tear to pieces by night.

How can God listen to such contradictory witness,

Unless He be pleased to decide on it in mercy?

Act and word manifest the secret thoughts and
    mind,

Both of them expose to view the veiled secret.

When your witnesses are purified they are accepted,

Otherwise they are arrested and kept in durance.

They enter into conflict with you, O stiff-necked one;

"Stand aloof and wait for them, for they too wait."⁹

Prayers for spiritual enlightenment (P. 399)

O God, who hast no peer, bestow Thy favour upon me;

Since Thou hast with this discourse put a ring in my ear,

Take me by the ear, and draw me into that holy assembly

Where Thy saints in ecstasy drink of Thy pure wine

Now that Thou hast caused me to smell its perfume,

Withhold not from me that musky wine, O Lord of faith!

Of Thy bounty all partake, both men and women,

Thou art ungrudging in bounties, O Hearer of prayer.

Prayers are granted by Thee before they are uttered,

Thou openest the door to admit hearts every moment!

How many letters Thou writest with Thy Almighty
    pen!

Through marvelling thereat stones become as wax.

Thou writest the *Nun* of the brow, the *Sad* of the eye,

And the *Jim* of the ear, to amaze reason and sense.

These letters exercise and perplex reason;

Write on, O skilful Fair-writer!

Imprinting every moment on Not-being the fair
    forms

Of the world of ideals, to confound all thought![10]

Yea, copying thereon the fair letters of the page of
    ideals,

To wit, eye and brow and moustache and mole!

For me, I will be a lover of Not-being, not of
    existence,

Because the beloved of Not-being is more blessed.[11]

God made reason a reader of all these letters,

To suggest to it reflections on that outpouring of
    grace.[12]

Reason, like Gabriel, learns day by day

Its daily portion from the "Indelible Tablet."[13]

Behold the letters written without hands on
    Not-being!

Behold the perplexity of mankind at those letters!
Every one is bewildered by these thoughts,
And digs for hidden treasure in hope to find it.

This bewilderment of mankind as to their true aims
is compared to the bewilderment of men in the dark
looking in all directions for the Qibla, and recalls the
text, ''O the misery that rests upon my servants.''[14]

Then follow reflections on the sacrifice by Abraham
of the peacock of ambition and ostentation. Next comes
a discourse on the thesis that all men can recognise the
mercies of God and the wrath of God; but God's mercies
are often hidden in His chastisements, and *vice versa*,
and it is only men of deep spiritual discernment who
can recognise acts of mercy and acts of wrath concealed
in their opposites. The object of this concealment is to
try and test men's dispositions; according to the text,
''To prove which of you will be most righteous in
deed.''[15]

Notes

1. Koran ii. 262.
2. Koran xv. 72.
3. Koran ix. 33.
4. Koran lxxiii. 20.

5. Koran xxxiii. 33.

6. Koran vii. 171.

7. "Islam is the baptism of God" (Koran ii. 132).

8. Koran xcii. 4.

9. Koran xxxii. 30. *I.e.,* Wait thou for their punishment, as they wait for thy downfall (Rodwell).

10. Here we have another Platonic doctrine. "Some say the belief of the Sufis is the same as that of the Ishraqin (Platonists)." Dabistan i Muzahib, by Shea and Troyer, iii. 281.

11. *I.e.,* I will recognise the nonentity of all this phenomenal being, and court self-annihilation.

12. The Bulaq translator renders *An naward* thus.

13. The "Indelible Tablet" (of God's decrees) is here applied to the Logos, – the channel through whom God renews the "world of creation" day by day.

14. Koran xxxvi. 29.

15. Koran lxvii. 2.

THE MAN WHO CLAIMED TO BE A PROPHET (P. 417)

A man cried out to the people, "I am a prophet; yea, the most excellent of prophets." The people seized him by the collar, saying, "How are you any more a prophet than we are?" He replied, "Ye came to earth from the spirit-world as sleeping children, seeing nothing of the way; but I came hither with my eyes open, and marked all the stages of the way like a guide." On this they led him before the king, and begged the king to punish him. The king, seeing that he was very infirm, took pity on him, and led him apart and asked him where his home was. The man replied, "O king, my home is in the house of peace (heaven), and I am come thence into this house of reproach." The king then asked him what he had been eating to make him rave as he did, and he said if he lived on mere earthly bread he should not have claimed to be a prophet. His preaching was entirely thrown away on worldly men, who only desire to hear news of gold or women,[1] and are annoyed with all who speak to them of the eternal life to come. They cleave to the present life so fast that they hate those who tell them of another. They say, "Ye are telling us old fables and raving idly;" and when they see pious men prospering they envy them, and, like Satan, become more opposed to them. God said, "What thinkest thou of him who holdeth back a servant of God when he prayeth?"[2] The king then said to him, "What is this inspiration of yours, and what profit do you derive from it?" The man answered, "What profit is there that I do not derive from it? I grant I am not rich in worldly wealth, yet the inspiration God teaches me is surely as precious as that which He taught the bees.[3] God taught them to make wax and honey, and He teaches me nobler things than these. Whoso has his face reddened with celestial wine is a prophet of like disposition with Muhammad, and whoso is unaffected by that spiritual drink is to be accounted an enemy to God and man."

The Prophet's prayer for the
envious people (P. 419)

O Thou that givest aliment and power and
  stability,

Set free the people from their instability.

To the soul that is bent double by envy

Give uprightness in the path of duty,

Give them self-control, "weigh down their
  scales,"[4]

Release them from the arts of deceivers.

Redeem them from envying, O gracious One,

That through envy they be not stoned like Iblis.[5]

Even in their fleeting prosperity, see how the
  people

Burn up wealth and men through envy!

See the kings who lead forth their armies

To slay their own people from envy!

Lovers of sweethearts have conceived jealousy,

And attempted one another's lives,

Read "Wais and Rámin" and "Khosrau and Shirin,"

To see what these fools have done to one another.

Lovers and beloved have both perished;
And not themselves only, but their love as well.
'Tis God alone who agitates these nonentities,
Making one nonentity fall in love with another.
In the heart that is no heart envy comes to a head,
Thus Being troubles nonentity.

This is followed by an anecdote of a lover who recounted to his mistress all the services he had done, and all the toils he had undergone for her sake, and inquired if there was anything else he could do to testify the sincerity of his love.

His mistress replied, "All these things you have done are but the branches of love; you have not yet attained to the root, which is to give up life itself for the sake of your beloved." The lover accordingly gave up life, and enjoyed eternal fruition of his love, according to the text, "O thou soul which art at rest, return to thy Lord, pleased, and pleasing Him."[6]

This is followed by a statement of the doctrine of the jurist Abu Hanífa, to whose school the poet belonged, that weeping, even aloud, during prayer does not render the prayers void, provided that the weeping be caused by thoughts of the world to come, and not by thoughts of this present world.[7] And, apparently in allusion to the name Abu Hanífa, the poet recalls the text, "They followed the faith of Abraham, the orthodox" (*Hanífun*).[8]

Notes

1. Koran iii. 12.
2. Koran xcvi. 9.
3. Koran xvi. 70.
4. Koran ci. 5.
5. Koran xv. 17. The sin of Iblis was his envy of Adam.
6. Koran lxxxix. 27.
7. Mishkát ul Masábih, i. p. 209, note.
8. Koran iv. 124.

THE SINCERE
REPENTANCE
OF NASÚH (P. 443)

A yáz, in weighing the pros and cons in regard to pardoning the courtiers, remarks that professions of faith and penitence when contradicted by acts are worthless, according to the text, "If ye ask them who hath created the heavens and the earth, they will say 'God;' yet they devise lies."[1] And in illustration of this he tells a story of a faithless husband who retired to a secret chamber ostensibly to say his prayers, but really to carry on an intrigue with a slave-girl, and the falsity of whose pretences was demonstrated by ocular proof of his condition. In like manner, on the day of resurrection man's hands and eyes and feet will bear witness against him of the evil actions done by him, thus confuting his pretences to piety. The test of a sincere repentance is abhorrence of past sins and utter abandonment of all pleasure in them, – the old love for sin being superseded by the new love for holiness.

Such a repentance was that of Nasúh. Nasúh in his youth disguised himself in female attire and obtained employment as attendant at the women's baths, where he used to carry on shameful intrigues with some of the women who frequented the bath. At last, however, his eyes were opened to the wickedness of his conduct, and he went to a holy man and besought him to pray for him. The holy man, imitating the long-suffering of the "Veiler of sins," did not so much as name his sin, but prayed, saying, "God give thee repentance of the sin thou knowest!" The prayer of that holy man was accepted, because the prayers of such an one are the same as God's own will, according to the tradition, "My servant draws nigh to me by pious works till I love him; and when I love him I am his ear, his eye, his tongue, his foot, his hand; and by me he hears, sees, talks, walks, and feels." Nasúh then returned to the bath a truly repentant man; but soon afterwards one of the women frequenting the bath lost a valuable jewel, and the king gave order that all persons connected with the bath should be stripped and searched. When the officers came to the bath to execute this order Nasúh was overwhelmed with fear, for he knew that if his sex were discovered he would certainly be put to death. In his fear he called upon God for deliverance, and swooned with fear and became beside himself, so that his natural self was annihilated, and he became a new creature, even as a corpse rising from the grave. When he came to himself he found that the lost jewel had been found, and those who had suspected him came and begged his pardon. Shortly afterwards the king's daughter sent for him to come and wash her head; but, in spite of her imperative commands, he refused to place himself again in the way of temptation, lest he might fall again, and God might "make easy to him the path to destruction."[2]

Man's members will bear witness against
him on the day of judgment, and confute
his claims to piety (P. 443)

On the resurrection day all secrets will be disclosed;
Yea, every guilty one will be convicted by himself.

Hand and foot will bear testimony openly
Before the Almighty concerning their owner's sins.
Hand will say, "I stole such and such things;"
Lip will say, "I asked for such and such things."
Foot will say, "I went after my own desires;"
Arm will say, "I embraced the harlot."
Eye will say, "I looked after forbidden things;"
Ear will say, "I listened to evil talk."
Thus the man will be shown to be a liar from head
    to foot,
Since his own members will prove him to be a liar.

Notes

1. Koran xxix. 61.
2. Koran xcii. 10.

THE MUSULMAN WHO
TRIED TO CONVERT
A MAGIAN (P. 460)

Musulman pressed a Magian to embrace the true
faith. The Magian replied, "If God wills it, no
doubt I shall do so."[1] The Musulman replied, "God
certainly wills it, that your soul may be saved from hell;
but your own evil lusts and the Devil hold you back."
The Magian retorted, using the arguments of the
Jabriyán or "Compulsionists," that on earth God is sole
sovereign, and that Satan and lust exist and act only in
furtherance of God's will. To hold that God is pulling
men one way and Satan another is to derogate from
God's sovereignty. Man cannot help moving in the
direction he is most strongly impelled to go; if he is
impelled wrongly he is no more to blame than a

building designed for a mosque but degraded into a fire-temple, or a piece of cloth designed for a coat but altered into a pair of trousers. The truth is, that whatever occurs is according to God's will, and Satan himself is only one of His agents. Satan resembles the Turkoman's dog who sits at the door of the tent, and is 'vehement against aliens, but full of tenderness to friends.''[2]

The Musulman then replied with the arguments of the *Qadarians* and *Mu'tazilites*, to prove the freedom of the will and consequent responsibility of man for his actions. He urged that man's free agency and consequent responsibility are recognised in common parlance, as when we order a man to act in a certain way, – that God expressly assumes man to be a free agent by addressing commands and prohibitions to him, and by specially exempting some, such as the blind,[3] from responsibility for certain acts, – that our internal consciousness assures us of our power of choice, just as outward sense assures us of properties in material objects, – and that it is just as sophistical to disbelieve the declarations of the interior consciousness, as those of the outward senses as to the reality of the material world.

He then told an anecdote of a man caught robbing a

garden and defending himself with the fatalist plea of irresponsibility, to whom the owner of the garden replied by administering a very severe beating, and assuring him that this beating was also predestined, and that he therefore could not help administering it. He concluded his argument by repeating that the traditions, "Whatever God wills is," and "The pen is dry, and alters not its writing," are not inconsistent with the existence of freewill in man. They are not intended to reduce good action and evil to the same level, but good actions will always entail good consequences, and bad actions the reverse.

A devotee admired the splendid apparel of the slaves of the Chief of Herat, and cried to Heaven, "Ah! learn from this Chief how to treat faithful slaves!" Shortly after the Chief was deposed, and his slaves were put to the torture to make them reveal where the Chief had hidden his treasure, but not one would betray the secret. Then a voice from heaven came to the devotee, saying, "Learn from them how to be a faithful slave, and then look for recompense."

The Magian, unconvinced by the arguments of the Musulman, again plied him with "Compulsionist" arguments, and the discussion was protracted, with the

usual result of leaving both the disputants of the same
opinion as when they began. The poet remarks that the
contest of the "Compulsionists" and the advocates of
man's free agency will endure till the day of judgment;
for nothing can resolve these difficulties[4] but the true
love which is "a gift imparted by God to whom He
will."[5]

Love puts reason to silence (p. 467)

Love is a perfect muzzle of evil suggestions;
Without love who ever succeeded in stopping them?
Be a lover, and seek that fair Beauty,
Hunt for that Waterfowl in every stream!
How can you get water from that which cuts it off?
How gain understanding from what destroys
  understanding?
Apart from principles of reason are other principles
Of light and great price to be gained by love of God.
Besides this reason of yours God has other reasons
Which will procure for you heavenly nourishment.
By your carnal reason you may procure earthly food,

By God-given reason you may mount the heavens.

When, to win enduring love of God, you sacrifice
reason,

God gives you "a tenfold recompense;"[6] yea, seven
hundred fold.

When those Egyptian women sacrificed their
reason,[7]

They penetrated the mansion of Joseph's love;

The Cup-bearer of life bore away their reason,

They were filled with wisdom of the world without
end.

Joseph's beauty was only an offshoot of God's
beauty;

Be lost, then, in God's beauty more than those
women.

Love of God cuts short reasonings, O beloved,

For it is a present refuge from perplexities.

Through love bewilderment befalls the power of
speech,

It no longer dares to utter what passes;

For if it sets forth an answer, it fears greatly

That its secret treasure may escape its lips.

Therefore it closes lips from saying good or bad,

So that its treasure may not escape it.

In like manner the Prophet's companions tell us,

"When the Prophet used to tell us deep sayings,

That chosen one, while scattering pearls of speech,

Would bid us preserve perfect quiet and silence."

So, when the mighty phœnix hovers over your head,[8]

Causing your soul to tremble at the motion of its wings,

You venture not to stir from your place,

Lest that bird of good fortune should take wing.

You hold your breath and repress your coughs,

So as not to scare that phœnix into flying away.

And if one say a word to you, whether good or bad,

You place finger on lip, as much as to say, "Be silent."

That Phœnix is bewilderment,[9] it makes you silent;

The kettle is silent, though it is boiling all the while.

Notes

1. Note the true believer is here represented as using the arguments of the *Qadarians* of *Mu'tazilites* for free will, as against the *Jabriyán* or fatalist argument put into the mouth of the Magian.

2. Koran xlviii. 29.

3. Koran xxiv. 60.

4. The Prophet said, "Sit not with a disputer about fate, nor converse with him."

5. Koran iii. 66.

6. Koran vi. 161.

7. "And when they saw him they were amazed at him, and cut their hands" (Koran xii. 31).

8. It is supposed to bring good fortune.

9. Bewilderment is the "truly mystical darkness of ignorance" which falls upon the mystic when the light of absolute Being draws near to him, and "blinds him with excess of light." See Gulshan i Raz, p. 13, and notes.

THE DEVOTEE WHO BROKE THE NOBLE'S WINE-JAR <small>(P. 471)</small>

A certain noble, who lived under the Christian dispensation when wine was allowed, sent his servant to a monastery to fetch some wine. The servant went and bought the wine, and was returning with it, when he passed the house of a very austere and testy devotee. This devotee called out to him, "What have you got there?" The servant said, "Wine, belonging to such a noble." The devotee said, "What! does a follower of God indulge in wine? Followers of God should have naught to do with pleasure and drinking; for wine is a very Satan, and steals men's wits. Your wits are not too bright already, so you have no need to render them still duller by drink." In illustration of this, he told the story of one Ziáyi Dalaq, a very tall man, who had a dwarfish brother. This brother one day received him very ungraciously, only half rising from his seat in answer to his salutation, and Ziáyi Dalaq said to him, "You seem to think yourself so tall that it is necessary to clip off somewhat of your height." Finally the devotee broke the wine-jar with a stone, and the servant went and told his master. The noble was very wrathful at the presumption of the devotee in taking upon himself to prohibit wine, as condemned by the law of nature, when it had not been prohibited by the Gospel, and he took a thick stick and went to the devotee's house to chastise him. The devotee heard of his approach and hid himself under some wool, which belonged to the ropemakers of the village. He said to himself, "To tell an angry man of his faults one needs to have a face as hard as a mirror, which reflects his ugliness without fear or favour." Just so the Prince of Tirmid was once playing chess with a courtier, and being checkmated, got into a rage and threw the chessboard at his courtier's head. So before playing the next game the courtier protected his head by wrappings of felt. Then the neighbours of the devotee, hearing the noise, came out and interceded for him with the noble, telling him that the devotee was half-witted, and could not be held responsible for his actions; and moreover, that as he was a favourite of God,[1] it was useless to attempt to slay him before his time, for the Prophet and other saints had been miraculously preserved in circumstances fatal to ordinary persons. The noble refused to be pacified; but the neighbours redoubled their entreaties, urging that he had so much pleasure in his sovereignty that he could well dispense with the pleasure of wine. The noble strenuously denied this, saying that no other pleasure of sovereignty, or what not, could compensate him for the loss of wine, which made him sway from side to side like the jessamine. The prophets themselves had rejected all other pleasures for that of spiritual intoxication, and he who has once embraced a living mistress will never put up with a dead one. The moral is, that spiritual pleasures, typified by wine, are not to be bartered away for earthly pleasures. The Prophet said, "The world is carrion, and they who seek it are dogs;" and the Koran says, "The present life is no other than a pastime and a sport; but the future mansion is life indeed."[2]

Description of a devotee who
trusted to the light of nature (P. 473)

His brain is dried up; and as for his reason,

It is now less than that of a child.

Age and abstinence have added infirmity to
    infirmity,

And his abstinence has yielded him no rejoicing.

He has endured toils, but gained no reward from his
    Friend;

He had done the work, but has not been paid.

Either his work has lacked value,

Or the time of recompense is not decreed as yet.

Either his works are as the works of the Jews,[3]

Or his reward is held back till the appointed time.

This grief and sorrow are enough for him,

That in this valley of pain he is utterly friendless.

With sad eyes he sits in his corner,

With frowning face and downcast looks.

There is no oculist who cares to open his eyes,[4]

Nor has he reason enough to discover the eye-salve.

He strives earnestly with firm resolve and in hope,

His work is done on the chance of being right.

The vision of "The Friend" is far from his course,

For he loses the kernel in his love for the shell.

Notes

1. Half-witted persons are supposed to be divinely protected.
2. Koran xxix. 64.
3. "But as to infidels, their works are like the mirage in the desert" (Koran xxiv. 39).
4. *I.e.*, he has no director (*Murshid i Kámil*) to instruct him in the right course.

BOOK VI

PROLOGUE (P. 492)

O life of the heart, Husámu-'d-Din,

My zeal burnt within me to write this sixth part!

The Mathnawi became a standard through thy
influence,

Thy sword (*Husam*) has made it an exemplar to the
world

O spiritual one, I now offer it to thee,–

This sixth part of the entire Mathnawi.

Enlighten the world's six sides with its six parts,

That it may illuminate him who is not illuminated!

Love has naught to do with five senses or six sides,

Its only aim is to be attracted to the Beloved!

But haply leave may be given me hereafter

To tell those mysteries so far as they can be told,

In a discourse more closely approximating to the
facts

Than these faint indications of those abstruse
matters.

Mysteries are not communicable, save to those who
know;

Mystery in the ear of infidels is no mystery.

Nevertheless, this is a call to you from God;

It matters not to Him whether ye accept or reject it.

Noah repeated His call for nine hundred years,

But his people only increased in rebellion.

Never did he draw back from admonishing them,

Never did he retire into the cave of silence.

He said, "At the barking and howling of the dogs

No caravan ever turned back in its road.

Nor does the full moon on a bright night cease
   shining

Because of the howling of dogs on earth.

The moon sheds her light, and the dogs howl;

Every one acts according to his nature.

To each one his office is allotted by the divine
   decree,

And he acts agreeably to his nature."

* * *

Art thou thirsting for the ocean of spirituality?

Disport thyself on this island of the Mathnawi!

Disport thyself, so long as thou seest every moment

Spiritual verities revealed in this Mathnawi.

When the wind blows the grass off the water,

The water then shows forth its own purity.

Behold the bright and fresh sprays of coral,

And the princely fruits growing in the water of life!

So, when the Mathnawi is purged of letters and
   words,

It drops all these, and appears as the sea of Unity.

Then speaker and hearer and spoken words

All three give up the ghost in that consummation.

Bread-giver and bread-eater and bread itself

Are purified of their forms and turn to dust.

But their essences in each of these three grades

Are distinguished, as in those states, so eternally.[1]

Their form turns to dust, but their essence not;

If one says it does, tell him it does not.

In the world of spirits all three await judgment,

Sometimes wearing their earthly forms, sometimes
   not.

The worth of a man depends on the
objects of his aspiration (P. 495)

One day a student asked a preacher,
Saying, "O most orthodox ornament of the pulpit,
I have a question to ask, O lord of learning;
Tell me the answer to it in this congregation.
A bird sat on the top of a wall;
Which was best, its head or its tail?"
He replied, "If its face was towards the town,
And its tail to the villages, then its face was best.
But if its tail was towards the town, and its face
Towards the villages, then prefer its tail to its face."
A bird flies with its wings towards its nest,
The wings of a man are his aspiration and aim.
If a lover be befouled with good and evil,
Yet regard not these; regard rather his aspiration.
Though a falcon be all white and unmatched in form,
If he hunts mice he is contemptible and worthless.
And if an owl fixes his affection on the king,
He is a falcon in reality; regard not his outward
    form.

Adam's clay was kneaded in the limits of a trough,

Yet he was exalted above heaven and stars.

"We have honoured Adam"[2] was not addressed to
   the sky,

But to Adam himself, full of defects as he was.

Did one ever propose to earth or heaven to receive

Beauty, reason, and speech and aspiration?[3]

Would you ever offer to the heavens

Beauty of face and acuteness of thought?

O son, did you ever present your silver body

As an offering to the damsels pictured on bath
   walls?

Nay, you pass by those pictures though fair as Huris,

And offer yourself sooner to half-blind old women.

What is there in the old women which the pictures
   lack,

Which draws you from the pictures to the old
   women?

Say not, for I will say it in plain words,–

'Tis reason, sense, perception, thought, and life.

In the old woman life is infused,

While the pictures of the bath have no life.

If the pictures of the bath should stir with life (soul),
They would uproot your love to all the old women.
What is soul? 'Tis acquainted with good and evil,–
Rejoicing at pleasant things, grieving at ills.
Since, then, the principle of soul is knowledge,
He who knows most is most full of soul.
Knowledge is the effect flowing from soul;
He who has most of it is most godlike.
Seeing then, beloved, that knowledge is the mark of
    soul,
He who knows most has the strongest soul.
The world of souls is itself entirely knowledge,
And he who is void of knowledge is void of soul.
When knowledge is lacking in a man's nature,
His soul is like a stone on the plain.
Primal Soul is the theatre of God's court,
Soul of souls the exhibition of God Himself.
All the angels were pure reason and soul,
Yet when the new soul of Adam came, they were as
    its body.
When in joy they crowded round that new soul,[4]
They bowed before it as body does before soul.

Notes

1. Koran xxxvi. 32: "But all gathered together shall be set before us."
2. Koran xvii. 72.
3. "We proposed to the heavens and to the earth to receive the deposit, but they refused the burden. Man undertook to bear it, but hath proved unjust and senseless" (Koran xxxiii. 72).
4. "We said unto the angels, 'Prostrate yourselves before Adam,' and they prostrated themselves, except Iblis" (Koran vi. 10).

THE DRUNKEN
TURKISH AMÍR AND
THE MINSTREL (P. 507)

Then follow exhortations to undergo "the pains of negation," as they are called in the *Gulshan i Raz*, – *i.e.*, even as the great saint and poet Faridu-'d-Din 'Attar cast away his drugs, to cast one's own will, knowledge, power, and "self" into the unique river of "annihilation,"[1] and from that state to rise to the higher state of eternal existence in God. The end and object of all negation is to attain to subsequent affirmation, as the negation in the creed, "There is no God," finds its complement and purpose in the affirmation "but God." Just so the purpose of negation of self is to clear the way for the apprehension of the fact that there is no existence but The One. The intoxication of life and its pleasures and occupations veils the Truth from men's eyes, and they ought to pass on to the spiritual intoxication which makes men beside themselves and lifts them to the beatific vision of eternal Truth. This is the same thing as saying they must pass on from negation to affirmation, from ignorance to the highest knowledge. This is illustrated by the story of the Turkish noble and the minstrel, which is given with an apology for using illustrations derived from drunkenness. A Turkish noble awoke from his drunken sleep, and called his minstrel to enliven him. The minstrel was a spiritual man, and proceeded to improve the occasion by singing a song with a deep spiritual meaning:–

"I know not if thou art a moon or an idol,
I know not what thou requirest of me.
I know not what service to pay thee,
Whether to keep silence or to speak.
Thou art not apart from me, yet, strange to say,
I know not where I am, or where thou art.
I know not wherefore thou art dragging me,
Now embracing me, and now wounding me!"

Thus the whole of his song consisted of repetitions of the words, "I know not." At last the noble could endure it no longer, and he took a stick and threatened to beat the minstrel, saying, "O wretch, tell us something you do know, and do not repeat what you do not know. If I ask you whence you come or what you have eaten, and you answer only by negations, your answer is a waste of time. Say what you mean by all these negations." The minstrel replied, "My meaning is a concealed one. I fear to make affirmations in opposition to your negations, so I state negations that you may get a hint of the corresponding affirmations from them. I now hint the truth to you in my song; and when death comes to you, you will learn the mysteries which at present I can only hint."

Spiritual mysteries set forth in the
Mathnawi under similes of intoxication (P. 507)

That wine of God is gained from *that* minstrel,[2]
This bodily wine from *this* minstrel.
Both of these have one and the same name in speech,
But the difference between their worth is great.

[169]

* * *

Men's bodies are like pitchers with closed mouths;
Beware, till you see what is inside them.
The pitcher of this body holds the water of life,
Whilst that one holds deadly poison.
If you look at the contents you are wise;
If you look only at the vessel you are misguided.
Know words resemble these bodies,
And the meaning resembles the soul.
The body's eyes are ever intent on bodies,
The soul's eyes on the reasonable soul;
Wherefore, in the figures of the words of the
    Mathnawi,
The form misleads, but the inner meaning guides.
In the Koran it is declared that its parables
"Mislead some and guide some."[3]
O God! when a spiritual man talks of wine,
How can a fellow spiritual man mistake his meaning?

* * *

Thus that minstrel began his intoxicating song,
"O give me Thy cup, Thou whom I see not!
Thou art my face; what wonder if I see it not?

Extreme nearness acts as an abscuring veil.[4]
Thou art my reason; what wonder if I see Thee not
Through the multitude of intervening obstacles?
Thou art 'nearer to me than my neck vein,'[5]
How can I call to Thee, 'Ho,' as if thou wert far off?
Nay, but I will mislead some by calling in the desert,
To hide my Beloved from those of whom I am
     jealous!"

This is illustrated by an anecdote of the Prophet and
'Ayísha. 'Ayísha was once sitting with the Prophet
without her veil, when a blind man came in. 'Ayísha,
knowing well the jealous disposition of her husband, at
once prepared to retire, on which the Prophet said, "The
man is blind and cannot see you." 'Ayísha replied by
signs that though the man could not see her she could
see him. Just so the spiritual man is jealous of exposing
his mysteries to the gaze of the profane, and from excess
of caution veils them in signs and hints.

Then comes a commentary on the tradition, "Die
before you die," *i.e.*, mortify your carnal passions and
lusts, and deny and annihilate your carnal "self" before
the death of the body overtakes you. Men who put off

repentance till they are at the point of death are likened to the Shi'as of Aleppo, who every year on the '*Ashura*, or tenth day of *Muharram,* meet at the Antioch gate to bewail the martyrdom of Hasan and Husain. Once, while they were thus engaged, a Sunni poet arrived at the city, and inquired the reason of this excessive grief and mourning. The Shi'as rebuked him for his ignorance of sacred history, and he said, "This martyrdom happened a long time ago; but it would seem, from your excessive grief, that the news of it has only just reached you. You must have been sleeping all this time not to have heard it before, and now you are mourning for your own sleepiness!" To the truly spiritual, who have drunk of God's wine and bear the "tokens of it on their foreheads,"[6] death is an occasion for rejoicing, not for wailing. The man who is engrossed with the trifling pleasures of the world and blind to the ample provision made for the soul is like an ant in a barn of wheat, toiling to carry off a single grain, when ample stores of wheat are already at its disposal. Spiritual men must continue urging the worldly to repent and avail themselves of this heavenly provision for their souls, careless, like Noah, whether their preaching is listened to or not. This is illustrated by an anecdote of a man who knocked at the door of an empty house at midnight, in order to give notice that it was time to prepare the meal taken at dawn in *Ramazan*.

Reason for knocking at the empty house (P. 512)

You have said your say; now hear my answer.
So as not to remain in astonishment and
    bewilderment.
Though to you this time seems midnight,
To me the dawn of joyful morn seems nigh.

*   *   *

To the vulgar all parts of the world seem dead,
But to God they are instinct with sense and love.
And as to your saying that "this house is empty,
Why then should I beat a drum before it?"
Know that the people of God expend money,
And build many mosques and holy places,
And spend health and wealth in distant pilgrimages,
In ecstatic delight, like intoxicated lovers;
And none of them ever say, "The Ka'ba is empty;"
How can one who knows the truth say that?

* * *

These people are ranged in battle array,
And risk their lives to gain God's favour;
One plunged in calamities like Job himself,
Another exhibiting patience like Jacob.
Thousands of them are thirsty and afflicted,
Striving in earnest desire to do God's will.
I likewise, in order to please the merciful God,
Beat my drum at every door in hope of dawn.
Seek ye a purchaser who will pay you gold;
Where will you find one more liberal than God?
He buys the worthless rubbish which is your
  wealth,
He pays you the light that illumines your heart.
He accepts these frozen and lifeless bodies of yours,
And gives you a kingdom beyond what you dream
  of.
He takes a few drops of your tears,
And gives you the divine fount sweeter than sugar.
He takes your sighs fraught with grief and sadness,
And for each sigh gives rank in heaven as interest.
In return for the sigh-wind that raised tear-clouds,

God gave Abraham the title of "Father of the
  faithful."

Come! in this incomparable and crowded mart

Sell your old goods and take a kingdom in payment!

Notes

1. Koran cxii. 4.
2. "A wine-cup tempered at the camphor fountain shall the
   just quaff" (Koran lxxvi. 5).
3. Koran ii. 24.
4. See couplet 122 of the Gulshan i Raz:—
   "When the object looked at is very close to the eye,
   The eye is darkened so that it cannot see it."
   I.e., When man is united with God he can no longer behold
   Him, for he is dwelling in Him.
5. Koran l. 15.
6. Koran xlviii. 29.

THE PURCHASE
OF BILÁL (P. 513)

To illustrate the rich recompense that is awarded to those who are faithful in tribulation, the story of Bilál is next recounted at length. Bilál was an Abyssinian slave belonging to a Jew of Mecca, and had incurred his master's displeasure in consequence of having embraced Islam. For this offence his master tortured him by exposing him to the heat of the midday sun, and beating him with thorns. But, notwithstanding his anguish, Bilál would not recant his faith, and uttered only the cry, "*Ahad, Ahad!*" "The One, the One God!" At this moment Abu Bakr, the "Faithful witness," happened to pass by, and was so struck by his constancy that he resolved to buy him off the Jew. After much higgling and attempts at cheating on the Jew's part he succeeded in doing so, and at once set him free.

When the Prophet heard of this purchase he said to Abu Bakr, "Give me a share in him;" but Abu Bakr told him, somewhat to his annoyance, that he had already set him free. Notwithstanding this Bilál attached himself to the Prophet, and was afterwards promoted to the honourable post of the Prophet's *Mu'azzin*.

This is followed by the story of Hilal, another holy man who, like Bilál and Luqman and Joseph, served a noble in the capacity of groom. His affections were set on things above, and he was ever pressing upwards towards the high mark of spiritual exaltation, and saying, like Moses, "I will not stop till I reach the confluence of the two seas, and for years will I journey on."[1] Herein he presented a great contrast to ordinary men, who are ever giving way to their lusts, and so being dragged down into the state of mere animals, or even lower. Hilal's master was a Musulman, yet one whose eyes were only partially open to the truth. He was in the habit of asking his guests their age; and if they answered doubtfully, saying, "Perhaps eighteen, or seventeen, or sixteen, or even fifteen," he would rebuke them, saying, "As you seem to be putting yourself lower and lower, you had better go back at once to your mother's womb." These guests are a type of men who lower themselves from the rank of humanity to that of animals. This master, however, was blind to Hilal's spiritual excellence, and allowed him to drag on a miserable existence in his stables. At last Hilal fell sick; but no one cared for him, till the Prophet himself, warned by a divine intimation, came to visit him, and commiserated his wretched condition. Hilal proved himself to be faithful through tribulation; for, instead of grumbling at his lot, he replied, "How is that sleep wretched which is broken by the advent of the Sun of prophecy? or how can he be called athirst on whose head is poured the water of life?" In truth, Hilal had by degrees become purified from the strain of earthly existence and earthly qualities, and washed in the fountain of the water of life, *i.e.*, the holy revelations of the Prophet, till he had attained the exalted grade of purity enjoined on those who would study God's Word aright.[2]

Growth in grace is accomplished by slow degrees, and not per saltum (P. 519)

Since you have told the story of Hilal (the new moon)
Now set forth the story of Badr (the full moon).

That new moon and that full moon are now united,

Removed from duality and defect and shortcomings.

That Hilal is now exalted above inward defect;

His outward defects served as degrees of ascension.

Night after night that mentor taught him grades of
    ascent

And through his patient waiting gave him
    happiness.

The mentor says, "O raw hastener, through patient
    waiting,

You must climb to the summit step by step.

Boil your pot by degrees and in a masterly way;

Food boiled in mad haste is spoiled.

Doubtless God could have created the universe

By the *fiat* 'Be!' in one moment of time;

Why, then, did He protract His work over six days,

Each of which equalled a thousand years, O disciple?

Why does the formation of an infant take nine
    months?

Because God's method is to work by slow degrees,

Why did the formation of Adam take forty days?

Because his clay was kneaded by slow degrees.

Not hurrying on like you, O raw one,
Who claim to be a Shaikh whilst yet only a child!
You run up like a gourd higher than all plants,
But where is your power of resistance or combat?
You have leant on trees or on walls,
And so mounted up like a gourd, O little dog rose;
Even though your prop may be a lofty cypress,
At last you are seen to be dry and hollow.
O gourd, your bright green hue soon turns yellow,
For it is not a natural but an artificial colour."

This is illustrated by an anecdote of an ugly old hag who painted her face to make it look pretty, but was detected and exposed to scorn.

Notes

1. Koran xviii. 59.
2. Koran lvi. 79.

STORY EIGHT

THE MAN WHO
RECEIVED A PENSION
FROM THE PREFECT
OF TABRIZ (P. 559)

These reflections on the nothingness of outward
form compared to spirit lead the poet to the
corollary that often men whose outward forms are
buried in the grave are greater benefactors to the poor
and helpless than men still living in the body. This is
illustrated by the story of the man who was maintained
by the Prefect of Tabriz. This man incurred heavy debts
on the credit of his pension, even as the Imam Ja'far
Sadiq was able to capture a strong fort single-handed
through the power of God assisting him. When the
creditors became pressing the man journeyed to Tabriz
to seek further aid; but on arriving there he found the

Prefect was dead. On learning this he was much cast down, but eventually recognised that he had erred in looking to a creature instead of his Creator for aid, according to the text, "The infidels equalise others with their Lord."[1] This obliquity of spiritual sight, causing him to see a mere human benefactor, where the real benefactor was God alone, is illustrated by anecdotes of a man buying bread at Kashan, of Sultan Khwarazm Shah deluded into misliking a fine horse by the interested advice of his Vazir, and of Joseph, who when imprisoned by Pharaoh was induced to trust for deliverance to the intercession of the chief butler rather than to God alone, for which cause "he remained several years in prison."[2] A charitable person of Tabriz endeavoured to raise funds for the poor man, and appealed to the citizens to aid him, but only succeeded in collecting a very small sum. He then visited the Prefect's tomb, and implored assistance from him; and the same night the Prefect appeared to him in a dream, and gave him directions where to find a great treasure, and directed him to make over this treasure to the poor man. Thus the dead Prefect proved a more liberal benefactor than the citizens of Tabriz who were still living.

The poor man's regrets for having placed
his trust in man and not in God (P. 561)

When he recovered himself he said, "O God,

I have sinned in looking for aid to a creature!

Although the Prefect showed great liberality,

It was in no wise equal to Thy bounty.

He gave me a cap, but Thou my head full of sense;

He gave me a garment, but Thou my tall form.

He gave me gold, but Thou my hand which counts it;

He gave me a horse, but Thou my reason to guide it;

He gave me a lamp, but Thou my lucid eyes;

He gave me sweetmeats, but Thou my appetite for
them;

He gave me a pension, but Thou my life and being;

His gift was gold, but Thine true blessings;

He gave me a house, but Thou heaven and earth;

In Thy house he and a hundred like him are
nourished.

The gold was of Thy providing, he did not create it;

The bread of Thy providing, and furnished to him
by Thee.

Thou also didst give him his liberality,

For thereby Thou didst augment his happiness.

I made him my *Qibla*, and directed my prayers to
him;

I turned away my eyes from Thee, the *Qibla*-maker!

Where was he when the Supreme Dispenser of faith

Sowed reason in the water and clay of man,

And drew forth from Not-being this heavenly dome,

And spread out the carpet of the earth?

Of the stars He made torches to illumine the sky.

And of the four elements locks with keys (of reason).

Ah! many are the buildings visible and invisible

Which God has made between heaven's dome and
earth.

Man is the astrolabe of those exalted attributes,

The attribute of man is to manifest God's signs.

Whatever is seen in man is the reflection of God,

Even as the reflection of the moon in water."

* * *

Say not two, know not two, call not on two!

Know the slave is obliterated in his lord!

So the lord is obliterated in God that created him;

Yea, lost and dead and buried in his Creator!

When you regard this lord as separate from God,

You annihilate at once text and paraphrase.

With eyes and heart look beyond mere water and
    clay,

God alone is the *Qibla*; regard not two *Qiblas*!

If you regard two you lose the benefit of both;

A spark falls on the tinder and the tinder vanishes!

Joseph kept in prison a long time
for having placed his hopes of release
in man and not in God (P. 567)

In like manner Joseph, in the prison,

With humble and earnest supplications

Begged aid, saying, "When you are released,

And are occupied with your ministrations to the
    king,

Remember me, and entreat the king

To release me too from this prison."

How can one prisoner fettered in the snare

Procure release for a fellow prisoner?

[185]

The people of the world are all prisoners,

Awaiting death on the stake of annihilation;

Except one or two rare exceptions,

Whose bodies are in prison but their souls in heaven.

Afterwards, because Joseph had looked to man for aid,

He remained in prison for many years.[3]

The Devil caused the man to forget Joseph,

And blotted Joseph's words from his remembrance;

And on account of this fault of that holy man

God left him in the prison for many years.

Notes

1. Koran vi. 1.
2. Koran xii. 42.
3. Koran xii. 42.